# ABOVE ALL

ABOVE PROGRAMS, POLITICS, PREFERENCES,
AND ALL OTHER PRIORITIES

# ABOVE ALL

## THE GOSPEL IS THE SOURCE OF
## THE CHURCH'S RENEWAL

# J. D. GREEAR

PUBLISHING
NASHVILLE, TENNESSEE

Published by B&H Publishing
Nashville, Tennessee

Dewey Decimal Classification: 234
Subject Heading: GOSPEL / SALVATION / GRACE
(THEOLOGY)

Front cover design and art direction by Jonathan C. Edwards.

1 2 3 4 5 6 7 • 23 22 21 20 19

*To the 1,102 Summit Network planters and international missionaries who have put comfort aside and left their homes because they believe the gospel really is above all.*

# ACKNOWLEDGMENTS

It's a bit of a shame that only one name ends up on the cover of most books. Anyone who has written a book knows it's a team effort. That has never been truer than with the book you hold in your hands.

Chris Pappalardo, The Summit's editor, has longed joked with me that his role is to make me sound like the best version of myself. He's said it so long that I've started saying it. And at this point, I don't think either of us is joking. I don't like me without him anymore. He's funneled all the energy from his days of being one of Duke University's "Cameron Crazies" into making the gospel clear and accessible.

Todd Unzicker has been leading the way in championing these ideas within the Southern Baptist Convention. I have been blown away by the sheer number of people he has talked to in order to make "gospel above all" a rallying cry for us. As I lead the SBC, I am led by Todd.

Jonathan Edwards—not the Puritan—applied his editorial hand to both the design and the content of this book. I don't know anyone else who can play both of those games like that. If there is any life or beauty in these pages, undoubtedly you'll find his fingerprints there.

At the eleventh hour, Katelyn Byram and Daniel Riggs helped me track down those niggling citations that were too slippery for my middle-aged mind. "I once heard it said" became a footnote with a citation. If anything is still amiss, that's on me.

Dana Leach has directed J. D. Greear Ministries (JDGM) now for two years. But I have grown so trusting of her leadership, it feels like it's been twenty. I'm praying for at least twenty (a *real* twenty, not a felt twenty) more years.

Speaking of JDGM, Michael Jongkind and Katie Persinger were indispensable during JDGM's launch, and they have kept that good ship steady ever since. I'd have sunk the boat five times already without them.

Aly Rand, my executive assistant with the New Joisey accent, has a large binder entitled, "How to Run J. D.'s Life." I'm not kidding. She doesn't know I found it. And run it she does. I'm convinced that as long as she is at the helm, I could go missing for about two to three months before our church would notice. If Aly went missing for a couple of minutes, everything would implode.

Devin Maddox, Taylor Combs, and the crew at B&H pushed to get these ideas into print harder than I did, and they have been the biggest believers in this book all along the way. It's hard to imagine a more encouraging publishing team.

Lastly, I would be remiss if I passed over my wife, Veronica, who consistently gives me the greatest gift an author can receive—a reminder that real life matters more. No one thinks I am more of a hero than Veronica, but at the same time, no one is less impressed that I write books. May God give everyone a blessing like that. And my four kids, Kharis, Allie, Ryah, and Adon are awesome. They love the ideas in these books and have cheered me on in writing them more than anyone. Love you guys.

# CONTENTS

# THE GOSPEL PRAYER

Because I am in Christ . . .

1. I have done nothing that could make you love me less, and nothing I could do that would make you love me more.

2. You are all I need for everlasting joy.

3. As you have been to me, so I will be to others.

4. As I pray, I'll do so according to the compassion you've shown at the cross and the power you demonstrated through the resurrection.

# CHAPTER 1

# GOSPEL
## ABOVE ALL

Bible-based Christianity is dead.

At least that's what society wants you to believe.

Churches are closing their doors. Evangelicals are leaving the faith. The tide of those who identify as "no religion" is rising.

Is the handwriting on the wall? Is the Christian movement done? Must Christians rethink their convictions?

It seems change is the only option.

We can't hope to reach the next generation with our Bible-thumping, worn-out doctrines of sin, the exclusivity of Christ, and our "archaic" notions of marriage and sexuality.

Change or embrace irrelevance.

And looking around, it seems a lot of Christians have gotten the message. Many have given up trying to maintain their historical Christian convictions.

> *Does God really believe that about marriage?*
> *Is the Bible really believable?*
> *Is church really all that important?*

For those that haven't given up on their beliefs, they've relegated their lives into the shadows. Hunkered down. Quarantined. Protected. Fighting to keep themselves and their children free from the infection of the culture that lurks about. They're no longer praying that Christ would use them to turn their worlds upside down like Peter did in those golden days of optimism. Not a chance. Peter didn't have to deal with the secular media. Or Hollywood. Or the LGBT agenda.

Instead they're praying that Christ would return within the hour and save them from the evil around them so that their troubles would be left behind. They might not get out much and engage with their neighbors in need of saving, but they will for sure mobilize to get to the voting booths. That's our last stand.

Go into these churches and ask the faithful attenders how a person can be saved, and you will likely get a biblically reliable answer. They know the Sunday school answer is Jesus. Ask them to explain the gospel, and they'll likely be two for two. This makes things interesting because I believe what the church—you and me—needs most in our present time is a recovery of *the gospel*.

> **How will the recovery of something we already know take us to places we've never been?**

But how will the recovery of something we already know take us to places we've never been? After all, isn't the proverbial definition of insanity doing the same things over and over again and expecting different results? For this reason we're tempted to think we need something new. We need something to change. We need a different method.

Isn't the real issue that we haven't mastered the new media of our hyper-technological age? Or that we need to update our politics to fit the twenty-first century?

Maybe it's a leadership crisis. After all, everything rises and falls on leadership! If seminaries would just train pastors to be better leaders, to staff to their weaknesses, to get more in touch with culture, and to understand and use their enneagram number, our churches would grow again. Right?

Sure—they might.

But with what type of growth?

All of these issues are important and deserve discussion, of course. But I contend that what we *really* need isn't anything new.

Jesus said his gospel—the events of God the Son coming to earth, living the life we were supposed to live, dying the death we were condemned to die, and rising from the dead to defeat sin and death and offer humanity a way to God through his sacrifice—contained such power that not even the gates of hell would be able to resist its advance.

Think about this: *The gospel is the one thing in the New Testament, other than Jesus himself, that is referred to directly as the power of God.*

Not *contains* the power of God.

Not *channels* the power of God.

The gospel *is* itself the raw, unstoppable, death-defeating power of God.

The apostle Paul explains in his letter to the Romans that the gospel is the power of God unto salvation for all who would believe (Rom. 1:16).

When dynamite was invented in the eighteenth century, its name was derived from the Greek word Paul uses in Romans 1 for power—*dunamis.*

Now, Paul, of course, didn't know anything about dynamite, but I think it's still a good image to use when thinking of the gospel. The gospel is God's power to create, to redeem, to heal, to bring back from the dead. It doesn't offer insights on a new or superior technique. It is raw, explosive power.

My dad told me that when he was a boy, one of the worst whoopins he got was when he broke into his dad's company's shed and "borrowed" some dynamite. He wanted to go fishing.

(I know that raises a lot of questions. Suffice it to say, we're fortunate to still have Dad around.)

As a boy, my dad may not have known about risk, but he knew something about power. Fishing sure is a lot easier when you do it with dynamite, Dad said. Toss the dynamite in the pond, wait for the BOOM, and then watch as lifeless fish float to the surface.

That's Western North Carolina fishing right there.

(He read over this chapter and asked me to make sure you knew he wasn't condoning this type of thing anymore.)

A stick of dynamite doesn't give you instructions on new ways to fish or tell you the best places to cast your line; it *is* the power that does all the work. In a similar way, the gospel doesn't give you instructions on how to change: it *is* itself the power to change.

This is the power the church needs.

And the most important question before us is this: How can we get the gospel back into the right place in the church?

The gospel is more important than our programs.

The gospel is more important than our preferences.

The gospel is more important than our priorities.

The gospel is more important than our politics.

The gospel is more important than _____.

It doesn't matter how you fill the blank; the gospel is always and will always be most important!

My guess is, if you picked up this book, you believe the gospel. You believe that God is holy and glorious and worthy and that you're sinful. You believe in what Jesus has done for you. But like many believers, when it comes to the pursuit of abundant *life*, you believe in other things as well. The gospel is one alternative among many.

Here's the reality: if the gospel is not above all, it loses its power to change us, our families, our neighborhoods, our places of work, and our world. In fact, if the gospel is not above all else, *it's not even the gospel anymore.*

We need the power of the gospel–the raw power of God–to bring transformation to every area of our lives. And then to our communities and our churches.

Let me speak a quick word of encouragement to the pastors and church staff members reading this. When the gospel is above all else in our churches,

> **If the gospel is not above all, it loses its power.**

our churches thrive. God's power in the gospel is such that it will make up for many of our shortcomings–our low budgets, our leadership deficiencies, our ministry misalignments, our political mistakes, and our strategic missteps. But when the gospel is *not* above all–when our focus is divided and we give priority elsewhere–expertise in all those things won't make much difference.

What the church needs now is what the church has always needed–a return to the gospel. This isn't nostalgia for a bygone age. I'm not, in the words of one pundit, "sacrificing the future in search of the past," and I'm not trying to make anything great again. What I am trying to do is show us that the only way to save the future is by going back to the very beginning.

This book is intended to be a wrenching look at how secondary things–quite often good things, sometimes even necessary things–have displaced the gospel as *the main focus* in the life of the church.

Martin Luther famously said that to progress in the Christian life is always to begin again. If we truly want to progress in our mission, we need to begin again with the gospel. We need to go back to the start. Back to where we first saw the glory of God's grace and mercy and love. Back to where Jesus humbled us, saved us, and gave us new life.

No matter what you've heard before, success is not found by being on the right side of history. True success–success that will never fail or fade—is found in being on the right side of gospel. Power is not found in the brilliance of a new strategy but in the emptiness of an ancient tomb.

## WHAT IS *THE GOSPEL*?

The word has been used so commonly for so long that it's become all but stripped of its meaning.

There's gospel-centered preaching, gospel-centered kids Sunday school, gospel-centered worship, gospel-centered tree and shrub removal. Okay, one of those I made up. (Maybe.) But "the gospel" has become shorthand for whatever is important to us in Christianity at the moment. It's also become a label we slap on things to assure newcomers that our church is hip, up-to-date, and theologically certified. But is that all the gospel has become?

A label?

What does it mean for the gospel to function as the power of God in our churches? If the gospel is truly God's raw power, we had better have it in the right place.

After Paul declares to the Romans that the gospel message is the power of God, he spends ten chapters explaining how the gospel works. We might summarize Paul's chapters by saying the gospel is the good news that:

> We were dead in our trespasses and sin.
>
> Religion couldn't help us.
>
> New resolutions to change couldn't help us.
>
> Jesus, the baby born of a virgin in Bethlehem, was the Son of God.
>
> He did what we couldn't do. He lived a righteous life that pleased God.
>
> Still he got crucified on a cross under the curse of sin.
>
> He did that for us.
>
> He died in our place.

But Jesus was raised from the grave to offer
new life in his Spirit.

Jesus gives this new life to all who call upon
him in faith.

The beauty of the gospel is that those who trust in Jesus need never again fear alienation from God. In Christ you are secure. In Christ you are loved. In Christ you are whole. In Christ you are chosen. In Christ you are pure. "Therefore, there is now no condemnation for those in Christ Jesus" (Rom. 8:1).

And now Christ has redeemed us to a life of a love and service where we can reflect to others what he has done in us.

Simply believing this, Paul says, releases into us the power of God to make it so. Renewing our minds in this message, he tells the Romans, transforms ordinary, sinful people into the kinds of people who accomplish the very will of God (Rom. 12:1–2).

In his letters to the Corinthians, Paul says the gospel's inherent power means there's nothing more important to talk about to the church than it. It is, literally, "in the first place." It is primary (1 Cor. 15:3–4).

Paul even goes as far to say there is nothing else he really cares about the people in his churches knowing. Christ and Christ crucified is enough (1 Cor. 2:2). He tells Titus, his young protégé, that the gospel of God's grace not only bestows forgiveness but all the power they need to live godly lives in this world (Titus 2:11–12). Believing the gospel is not only how you get released from the *penalty* of sin, it's how you get released from the *power* of sin, also.

Because of the unparalleled power of the gospel, it is not something the biblical writers expect us to learn on the Romans Road and then leave behind. It contains everything necessary for success in the Christian life.

It's not just the 101 class of a four-year Christianity major.

Not just the diving board off of which we jump into the pool of Christianity.

Not just the milk that nourishes us until we are mature enough for meat.

The gospel *is* the meat.

And the dessert too, for that matter.

More than just the 101 introductory class to Christianity, it's the entire campus at which classes are held.

More than just the diving board, it's the whole pool.

The way you grow in Christ is the way you began in Christ: faith in the finished work and the empty tomb. To progress is always to begin again.

Peter says the gospel is so profound the angels, who stand around the throne of God every day, long to just catch a glimpse of it (2 Pet. 1:11–12). How hard must it be to impress an angel? They understand more theology than we ever will during our lifetimes. They had front row seats to God's mind-bending creative power that spun billions of stars into space. They saw God split the Red Sea and fill Balaam's donkey's mouth with words and sentences. They are themselves so powerful that a mere look at them turns the strongest human into a quivering puddle of fear. Yet these angels are still blown away by the simple gospel message. They want nothing more than to delve more deeply into it.

The beauty of the gospel is endless because the beauty of God is endless.

> **The beauty of the gospel is endless because the beauty of God is endless.**

This means that wherever you are in your journey with Christ—whether you're in doubt that Jesus really is who he says he is or you've been convinced of the gospel's power for seventy years—you're just getting started. And the great news for each of us is that, as Peter says, embedded in the gospel are all the resources you need to become everything God wants you to be (2 Pet. 1:3).

Tragically, a lot of Christians have moved on from it.

I was once at a conference where the speaker before me explained that the church had heard enough about the death of Jesus. He said (and I wrote it down word for word because I couldn't believe it), "We need to stop talking so much about Jesus' death. Everyone already freakin' knows about that. We need to talk now about his life."

The apostle Paul would never had said such a thing. And not just because he would avoid dirty words like *freakin'*. No, Paul knew that the only way to understand Jesus' life and experience his power as our own is to lean more fully and deeply into his death.

A brief note here: What are you supposed to do when you are an invited guest and the speaker before you says something like that? Typically, I prefer to honor the role of "guest" and let the conference host answer to God for what has been said.

Typically.

But when dealing with an issue of first importance—*the* issue of first importance—I had to throw my hat in the ring. I said, "Respectfully, I would encourage you never to do what the previous speaker has told you to do."

Yep. I did that.

And it was as awkward as you're imagining it.

Worth it.

### More Than Just "God Loves You"

I haven't been in school for years, but I still have nightmares about being unprepared for a final exam—showing up only to find out that *today* is the day 80 percent of my grade is determined and that I had forgotten all about it.

Imagine with me: your professor announces that your final exam is to write an essay identifying the three different kinds of atomic isotopes and discussing the varying electromagnetic qualities distinguishing them. The thing is, you don't have the foggiest idea what he is talking about—you vaguely remember some song about being home on the range where the deer and the isotope play, but you're pretty sure he's talking about something else.

Fast-forward ninety painful minutes, and you take the long, lonely walk up to the professor's desk at the front of the auditorium. You reach out to turn in your failing essay.

But then something happens.

Just as the pages of your scribbled nonsense are about to hit the professor's inbox, a classmate that you have never met reaches out, grabs your exam, marks out your name, and prints his own name. Then he writes *your* name on *his* exam. Then he turns both in.

The grades come back.

You pass.

He fails.

You get credit for his and he takes the blame for yours.

Now, I realize you're not allowed to actually do this in college, but it's a good picture of what Jesus did for us in the thirty-three years he spent on earth. He lived the life you were supposed to live and then erased his name and wrote yours on it. He died the death you were condemned to die, wiping out your name and writing his. His obedience covers what you couldn't and didn't do. His reward comes to you. Your punishment goes to him. This is what Christian theologians call the Great Exchange.

The gospel is not just the message that God loves you. He absolutely does, of course, and if he didn't, there would be no gospel. But he shows you the length, breadth, and height of his love through the beauty of *substitution*.

Don't miss that word. This word is vital to the gospel, for without substitution there would be no gospel.

At The Summit Church in North Carolina, where I have been privileged to pastor for almost twenty years, we summarize the gospel in these four words:

Jesus in my place.

You might think of it this way: Jesus did not just die *for* you; he died *instead of* you. He suffered your curse so you could inherit his righteousness (Gal. 3:13). He was clothed with shame so you could sit at the seat of honor (Heb. 12:2). He was struck down so you could be lifted up (Isa. 53:3–4). The Father turned his face away from Jesus so that he could turn his face toward you (Matt. 27:46). He lived the life you were supposed to live and died the death you were condemned to die so that you could have the reward he deserved—eternal life in the presence of God (Col. 3:4).

The prophet Isaiah predicted this holy substitution more than seven hundred years before it happened.

> He himself bore our sicknesses, and he carried our pains; but we in turn regarded him stricken, struck down by God, and afflicted. But he was pierced because of our rebellion, crushed because of our iniquities; punishment for our peace was on him, and we are healed by his wounds. We all went astray like sheep; we all have turned to our own way; and the LORD has punished him for the iniquity of us all. (Isa. 53:4–6)

Jesus' act of substitution is what separates Jesus' gospel from every other religion of the world. I've heard it said that it's possible to spell every other religion in the world "D-O." *Do this. Don't do that. Go here. Say this. Rub this. Touch that. Pray this. Chant that.* If you do these things often enough and well enough, so other religions say, God will accept you.

At least you hope.

The gospel, on the other hand, is spelled "D-O-N-E." Jesus did everything necessary to save us. In his final moments on the cross, Jesus cried out, "It is finished!" Not, "I got it started, now you take over." All the *doing* necessary to save has already been *done*.

In every other religion, God sends prophets as teachers who reveal a plan to earn God's favor; in Christianity the greatest Prophet is not merely a teacher but a Savior who has earned God's favor for you and gives it to you as a gift.

Let that sink in. In Christ you don't have to work to please God or to appease his anger or disappointment. The doing we do is done as a grateful response to what has been done on our behalf and in our place.

Our good works flow from salvation, not in pursuit of it.

Tim Keller says it like this: "Every other religion teaches, 'I obey; therefore I am accepted.' The gospel declares, 'I am accepted; therefore I obey.'"[1]

This is the good news—the power of God in the gospel—that saves us. This good news is more important than anything else, and not just because it obtains for us eternal life. The gospel does so much more than just that. The gospel is the source of our life—here, now, and to come. It is itself the power of God.

Because of this, it should be above all.

Most churchgoing folk, if asked about the gospel, know this. They can tell you about substitution, sometimes even about "do" versus "done." In fact, they may be able to articulate it better than me. But that doesn't mean the gospel occupies the right place in their hearts, lives, or worldviews.

Christians often see the gospel only as baby food. The starting point. The entry rite into Christianity. The prayer we pray to begin our relationship with Jesus.

But the gospel *is* the Christian life! It is not just the ABCs of Christianity; it is the A–Z. All of the Christian life flows from the good news of what Jesus has done on the cross. The gospel is the place we stay and never get tired of. The place we never stop learning, growing, and living.

That's why growth in Christ is never about going *beyond* the gospel but going deeper *into* the gospel. The gospel is like a well. The purest waters are found when you go deeper, not wider.

Of the 538 different variations of Batman my generation has had to endure, I think Christopher Nolan's 2005 megahit,

*Batman Begins,* is the best one. In it, young Bruce Wayne falls down an old well that apparently had been covered up for years. The surrounding brush had grown over so much that the opening to the well was completely invisible. It wasn't until years later that Bruce returned to the well. What he found was it was actually the entry to a vast, underground cave with unspeakable treasures and the secrets to becoming "the Batman."

There was so much more to Wayne Manor than what could be found above ground. To experience the full riches of the Wayne family estate, one needed to go deeper.

This is how we must treat the gospel.

We may think we see and understand all that's on the surface of the gospel message, but there's more to be discovered in the depths.

The more we look, the more we're transformed. The more we discover, the more we see. The apostle Paul says we grow spiritually as we gaze into God's glory (2 Cor. 3:18). As we behold the glory of Christ in the gospel, we become more like him. We grow from glory to glory.

Think about your own journey with Christ. How did you first become a Christian? You beheld the glory of God in the good news of what Jesus had *done* for you.

And now, how do you, as a Christian, become more and more like Jesus? By continuing to gaze at the glory of the God who did these things for you. By believing it remains finished.

Just as we are *saved* by believing the gospel and beholding Jesus with eyes of wonder, so we are *sanctified* in the same way. The gospel gets us in, and the gospel gets us all the way home.

Which is why we *all* still need it.

And why we need it more than anything else.

### Of First Importance?

Evangelical Christians have always been gospel people, of course. After all, it's in our very name. The word *evangelical* is a transliteration of the Greek word *gospel*. So in that sense the gospel has always been our "brand." It's been the heart of Christianity from the beginning. It's what gives our faith life.

But now it seems like we are tempted to turn elsewhere for renewal and for life.

> You foolish [Evangelicals]! Who has cast a spell on you? . . . Are you so foolish? After beginning by the Spirit, are you now finishing by the flesh? (Gal. 3:1–3)

Our failure to see renewal isn't a result of holding the gospel so tightly that we're rusty on modern techniques. Rather, it's a result of holding techniques too tightly and getting rusty with the gospel. We've removed the gospel from its place of first importance. It no longer is supreme. It no longer is our first priority.

We must turn *back* to the gospel of God's grace in Jesus if we want to go forward in mission.

None of our goals for personal growth will take off without the gospel. None of our calls for renewal will endure if they are not grounded in the gospel. The fire "to do" in the Christian life comes only from being soaked in the fuel of what has been *done.*

A quick note to my fellow pastors: this has to start in the pulpit. Every sermon should be grounded in the good news of what Jesus Christ has done. Charles Spurgeon once said that in every one of his sermons, he would "plow a trough" back to Jesus. I used to think that meant he thought we should give a gospel invitation at the end of every talk. But Spurgeon meant more than that. Spurgeon meant that the water of life necessary to do whatever the Scriptures commanded us to do flowed only from the finished work of Christ. Apart from faith in that, we preach a powerless religion, and our calls for renewal—however creative, innovative, and winsome—are as dead as the stone tablets in Moses's hands. Every story, every command, every principle in Scripture should point to the finished work of Christ. If we don't do this, we remove the *life* from the Book of Life.

Since Jesus claimed all of the Scriptures point to him (Luke 24:27), this shouldn't be too difficult for us. Just as the point of the Bible is to exalt his name, the point of every sermon should be the same.

To paraphrase D. Martyn Lloyd-Jones, the goal of a lecture is that people leave with *information*; the goal of a motivational speech is that they leave with *action steps*; the goal of a sermon is that people leave *worshipping*. Gospel preaching will always have Christ-exalting worship as its aim.

When people in our communities think about and talk about us, they should think and talk about the gospel. It should be both the ultimate point and the basis of every ministry and endeavor of our churches.

Think about your own church for a moment: what's the one thing your church is about?

Is the gospel what you leave your church talking about?

Or do you talk about your pastor's insights, your great worship band, your guest services, your massive pipe organ, your care for the poor, or your courageous proclamations against sin? Do others see your church as that place that gives really practical, helpful advice about life? Or as a classroom with theologically robust, original-languages-savvy preaching?

There is nothing wrong with most of these things, but none of them *are* the power of new life. They can be means of responding to or living out the power of God, but none of them *are* the raw power of God. Only the gospel, according to Scripture, *is* power.

Apart from the gospel, our ingenious life-change strategies will lack staying–and saving–power. Apart from the gospel our kindness to the poor will only make people comfortable for a while before they perish eternally. Apart from the gospel, the world we reshape through our politics will be every bit as bad as the one we are trying to reform. Apart from the gospel, self-help strategies will only lead us to pride (if we succeed) or despair (if we fail). After all, "Ten Steps Toward a Healthy Marriage" won't transform your marriage nearly as much as learning, understanding, and meditating on the ten *billion* steps Jesus took toward you will.

What does this mean for us and our churches? It means it's possible to lead people astray not just by teaching wrong things but also by giving true things—good things—too prominent a place.

We've covered your church, but what about you? What's the one thing you are about? What is of first importance to you? Are you leading others astray by putting emphasis where it doesn't belong?

The devil would like nothing more than to divide and distract us with secondary matters.

> **We have a gospel too great and a mission too urgent to be distracted by any secondary thing.**

We have a gospel too great and a mission too urgent to be distracted by any secondary thing. Everything we do in our own lives and in our churches must be run through the filter of how well it enables and deepens our gospel mission.

## ABOVE ALL: WHERE THIS BOOK IS HEADED

What would happen if we returned the gospel to its rightful place in our lives and churches?

I'm convinced we'd see a renewal of God's presence and power through this people. That's how it happened in the nation of Israel. When they "remembered" the kindnesses of God to them, the nation awakened and experienced God's blessing. When they forgot, they descended into chaos (for example, see Deut. 4:9, Judg. 8:34, and Isa. 65:11).

That's what this book is about—helping us *remember*.

We want to remember the greatness of the gospel in such a way that it becomes of *first importance, above all* else.

Here's what I think that will look like in practice—our roadmap for the remainder of this book.

### Gospel Change

The gospel will not be presented as merely the entry rite of our faith journey but the focus of our faith for the entirety of our Christian life. People will not leave our worship services or Bible studies overwhelmed by all the things they need to do for God but in awe of what he has done for them and promises to do through them.

### Gospel Mission

Making disciples will be the central, defining mission of the church. The list of good things Christians and churches can do is long, but good things can divert us from the one central mission Christ gave his church: make disciples (Matt. 28:18–20). We won't cease doing everything else; we'll just bring every other assignment into service of our central commission.

### Gospel Multiplication

The focus of our ministries will be empowering ordinary members to be the tip of the gospel spear in their communities. This is what characterized the early church and what has been true of the church whenever and wherever we find it expanding rapidly.

### Gospel Hope

The gospel compels eternal optimism. Not the facile, whimsical, personality-driven kind but the deep-seated conviction that God's plans for the world are as hopeful as the empty tomb declares they are. The future, William Carey said, is as bright as the promises of God. When the gospel is above all, hope for and excitement about the future will define the church, no matter how dark the day seems to us.

### Gospel Grace

Those who truly believe the gospel become like the gospel. When the gospel is above all, the generosity of our spirit will match the graciousness of our message. Our teaching should merely explain with words a grace that people already see modeled by our lives. This generosity of spirit not only shapes the way we relate to people on the outside; it impacts how we treat one another too.

### Gospel above My Culture

If the gospel is above all, we find a unity in it greater than the myriad of things from our heritages that might divide us. We'll always feel a natural affiliation with people of our own ethnicity and culture, with those who share similar backgrounds to us, and with those whose way of life is similar to ours. But the gospel will be larger in our hearts than even those things, and thus we'll feel *more* kinship, a *deeper* affiliation with believers whose culture differs from ours than we do with people from our own culture who don't share our passion for the gospel. This should empower the church to achieve a unity between ethnicities that our society longs for but is unable to obtain.

### Gospel above My Preferences

When the gospel is above all, we will eagerly sacrifice our preferences for the sake of the Great Commission. Like Paul, we'll wear our preferences like a garment we are ready to shed for the sake of the Great Commission whenever necessary. The question we bring to church will not be, *What kind of church do I prefer?* but, *What type of ministry best reaches the people in this community?*

### Gospel above My Politics

And just when you thought the book was salty enough, we'll ask how the gospel being above all should transform our approach to politics. We'll see that when the gospel is above all, every other agenda—especially political ones—take a distinct secondary place to it. This is not to say that politics aren't important or that Christians shouldn't engage in them, nor is it to say that Christians should avoid controversial issues and "just preach Jesus." Quite the contrary—the gospel often compels us to speak out. But when the gospel is above all, we'll do so in a way that keeps the gospel central.

We'll find that when the gospel is above all in our churches, just as Jesus gathered disciples of different political persuasions, so will we. And we'll see that if that's not happening, we have good reason to question whether the gospel really is as prominent in our churches as we think it is.

## WE'RE BACK

Our culture might believe that Christianity has one foot in the grave, but we shouldn't be intimidated. "Prophetic" voices declaring the imminent doom of our faith aren't new. We can't let doubt, distraction, or despair cause us to drift away from the hope of the gospel and the belief that God is still moving.

Because he is.

Disconnecting our lives and our faith from the gospel disconnects us from him, however, and that does mean certain death.

Be encouraged: from the very birth of our faith, the empire has been saying the days are numbered for followers of Jesus. The French philosopher Francois-Marie Arouet (1694–1778), better known by his pen name Voltaire (though he sounds so much less intimidating as Francoi-Marie!), famously predicted that Christianity would be dead within a hundred years of his death. By the 1880s, he wrote, "There will not be a Bible in the earth except one that is looked upon by an antiquarian curiosity seeker."

More recently, *TIME* magazine ran a cover story on April 8, 1966, famously posing the question, "Is God Dead?" They assumed the answer was obvious. If not dead, at least ready for hospice.

But here we are, more than 250 years removed from Voltaire and more than fifty years from the *TIME* cover. God is not only not dead; his church is growing, and his Spirit is moving. Voltaire, on the other hand, is dead. And while *TIME* magazine may still be sputtering along, more than once investors have thought about calling in hospice.

Paul wrote to the church at Colossae two thousand years ago encouraging them that the same gospel that had come to them was now expanding all over the world and transforming lives everywhere it went (Col. 1:6).

That's still true.

A friend of mine says, "If you're not dead, God's not done."

We're not dead, and God's not done with us, either.

Last year more people became Christians than any year to date. More Muslims have converted to Christianity in the last fifteen years than in the entire thirteen centuries since Islam's conception. The global South has seen a remarkable increase in evangelical Christianity in the twenty-first century. People are being saved by the thousands in South America, Africa, and Asia. Even in the West, where the numbers of evangelicals are declining, we're not witnessing the death of true Christianity but of cultural Christianity, which was never gospel Christianity to begin with. And in some of the most difficult places in the Western world, in some of our darkest corners, the church is growing. And thriving.

We don't need another Savior.

We don't need another focus.

We don't need a different power.

There is one name under heaven given among men by which we must be saved (Acts 4:12).

There is one source to which we turn for God's power.

His name is Jesus.

Faith in his finished work overcomes the world. We must, therefore, be resolved with Paul to know nothing but Christ and him crucified and to let the gospel occupy the place of first importance in every facet of our lives.

It must always remain *above all*.

Now let's talk about how we do this.

# CHAPTER 2

# **GOSPEL** CHANGE

*"Don't you know, young man, that from every*
*town, and every village, and every little hamlet in*
*England, wherever it may be, there is a road to*
*London? . . . And so from every text in Scripture,*
*there is a road to the metropolis of the Scriptures*
*that is Christ. And my dear brother, your business is*
*when you get to a text, to say, 'Now what is the road*
*to Christ?' and then preach a sermon, running along*
*the road towards the great metropolis—Christ. And I*
*have never yet found a text that had not got a road*
*to Christ in it, and if I ever do find one that has*
*not a road to Christ in it, I will make one; I will go*
*over hedge and ditch but I would get at my Master."*
—Charles Spurgeon

Most of us aren't scared to go to church.

Maybe a little nervous. Perhaps you're worried that your
kids are going to misbehave and embarrass you. Or that you'll

end up near that lady who refuses to take her screaming baby out to the lobby. Or that your pastor will do that little thing where he closes his notebook and starts "just sharing." Right through lunch and kickoff.

Or maybe you're nervous that it will be crowded and you'll have to park near the back of the lot and walk that long 120 yards to the worship center. In the rain. And Brother Fred who drives the little golf cart shuttling people back and forth from their cars might get tied up with senior adults again and not get to you. Again.

But the truth is, these are likely the extent of your fears.

For many Christians around the world, though, this is not the case. Sam James, the man who, fifty-six years ago, planted the church I pastor today, told me about church services in Vietnam, where he has lived as a missionary for the last five decades, where they would begin services each Sunday unsure if Communist officials would *again* break in mid-service (or suddenly stand up in the service revealing themselves) and drag their leaders off to prison.

Suddenly those 120 yards to the worship center don't seem that long.

Another friend of mine leads a house church in a Muslim region of Central Asia. He told me that after going through a season where the church was not growing, he asked members to write down five names of people whom they knew needed to hear the gospel of Jesus. He then asked them to identify the name of the person on that list who was the least likely to kill them if they shared Jesus with them. *That* would be the one they would pray about reaching out to that week.

Okay, I guess missing kickoff wasn't the end of the world.

As I write this chapter, reports have been coming out of China of increased government pressure on evangelical churches. This report came from *Christianity Today:* "Beijing authorities threatened to close Zion Church last month after the fifteen-hundred-member congregation . . . refused to install surveillance cameras in its sanctuary."[1]

Recently revised government regulations on religious groups have led to the burning of crosses, replacing them with Chinese flags, and forcing religious groups to remove Christian imagery from their church buildings. In some cases state officials and police have sought to track down churchgoers and attempt to prevent them from gathering together.

The screaming kid in the lobby is still annoying, but I can deal.

The early church began amid the same type of terrifying national and religious hostility. Throughout the entire book of Acts, we see both religious and secular powers trying to stamp out the expansion of Jesus' gospel movement. Jesus and his followers brought a life-giving—but unwanted—revolution. Jewish religious leaders and Roman government officials didn't agree on much, but they were united in the conviction about the need to squelch Christians, their gospel, and their sensational stories about Jesus of Nazareth. In nearly every one of the first eight chapters of Acts, we are told about plots to destroy the church. And in Acts 8 we're introduced to a man named Saul who makes it his life mission to end faith in Jesus.

Saul was ruthless.

Saul went to every house on the block, and wherever he found Christians, he dragged them out of their homes and threw them in prison (Acts 8:3). Saul even saw his persecution of the early Christians as a service to God:

> For you have heard about my former way of life in Judaism: I intensely persecuted God's church and tried to destroy it. I advanced in Judaism beyond many contemporaries among my people, because I was extremely zealous for the traditions of my ancestors. (Gal. 1:13–14)

Read that again.

Saul would stop to meditate on Scripture and sing psalms before he broke their doors in. He even thought his zeal for this gave him reason to *boast* before God:

> If anyone thinks he has grounds for confidence in the flesh, I have more: circumcised the eighth day; of the nation of Israel, of the tribe of Benjamin, a Hebrew born of Hebrews; regarding the law, a Pharisee; regarding zeal, persecuting the church; regarding the righteousness that is in the law, blameless. (Phil. 3:4–6)

Saul felt good about himself. But then something happened he did not expect or even think possible. Saul *saw something.*

Take a look at Acts 9:

> Now Saul was still breathing threats and murder against the disciples of the Lord. He went to the high priest and requested letters from him to the synagogues in Damascus, so that if he found any men or women who belonged to the Way, he might bring them as prisoners to Jerusalem. As he traveled and was nearing Damascus, a light from heaven suddenly flashed around him. Falling to the ground, he heard a voice saying to him, "Saul, Saul, why are you persecuting me?"
>
> "Who are you, Lord?" Saul said.
>
> "I am Jesus, the one you are persecuting," he replied. "But get up and go into the city, and you will be told what you must do." (vv. 1–6)

Saul hated Christians.

He threatened Christians.

He harassed Christians.

He murdered Christians.

But then, all at once, Saul switched teams. Now?

Saul sought to turn everyone who wasn't a Christian already *into* one (Acts 9:20).

Saul's whole Damascus road episode couldn't have lasted more than a few moments, but it changed everything in his life, forever. In an instant Saul went from murderous persecutor to grateful servant. That didn't happen after listening to a lecture. He wasn't given a list of compelling, practical, life-improving action steps. What Saul heard doesn't even appear to have been alliterated.

Saul was given a vision of incredible power and unthinkable grace.

*Before the gospel*, Saul took life in the name of God. After the gospel, he offered his own life as a sacrifice. His life focus went from "serve God and kill" to "serve God and die."

*Before the gospel*, pride in his religious obedience meant everything to him. After the gospel, humility arising from the awareness of what God had done for him consumed every part of who he was. (You can read about this in Philippians 3:7–8. The actual Greek word Saul uses to describe his feelings toward his religious accomplishments is *skubala*. Our English Bibles politely translate it as "rubbish" or "dung," but it was the kind of word that caused first-century moms to scrub out their middle-school boys' mouths with soap.)

*Before the gospel*, Paul was known as Saul, the namesake of Israel's proud, tall, good-looking, self-willed, and self-sufficient king. After the gospel, he was known as Paul, a name that literally means "small" or "humble."

Saul the mighty became Paul the dependent.

*Before the gospel*, Paul seethed with jealousy and hatred (Rom. 7:1–7). After the gospel, he proclaimed himself the chief of sinners and declared that his heart was so broken over his lost friends that if he could, he would go to hell if it meant they could go to heaven (Rom. 9:1–3).

Talk about humility.

Talk about zeal.

Talk about love.

In a mere moment Paul changed.

No wonder he said, "For I am not ashamed of the gospel, because *it is the power of God* for salvation to everyone who believes, first to the Jew, and also to the Greek" (Rom. 1:16, emphasis added).

The raw power that raised Christ from the dead is the same power that raised Saul from deathly pride to life-giving humility.

Powerful indeed.

## THE POWER THAT CHANGES US

You may not think of yourself as a boastful person. But you are.

I'm not saying that because I've done surveillance on you. I'm saying that because we *all* boast in something. We are always searching for something that sets us apart from others.

We boast in what we turn to for security. Whatever we turn to when the chips are down, to tell us, "Everything is going to be okay." Whatever we think guarantees that good things will be ahead for us. Whatever tells us that we are good, acceptable people and that our lives will be approved by whoever's opinion matters to us.

Some people boast in how talented or beautiful they are. Others boast in how much they know. Some in what they own or how much they've accomplished. Some in how morally good they are. Some in the strength of their families.

Paul experienced some of those things, but he told the Galatians that he would never again boast about anything besides the gospel—a message that declared that Paul was such a miserable wreck that the Son of God had to endure a bloody death just to keep him out of hell (Gal. 6:14).

Paul boasted in his shame.

Paul's boast in the gospel is like sitting in a room of millionaires and boasting about your collection of food stamps.

My family loves the comedian Brian Regan. Almost every family night includes us watching one of his sketches. One of our favorites is about the "Me Monster." You know, the guy at the party who manages to turn the focus of every conversation toward himself. No matter what you've done, he's done something better.

Brian wishes he had the chance to walk on the moon because then, he says, he'd always have a retort for the me monster. "Oh yeah, well I walked on the moon." Because, you know, nothing beats walking on the moon.

Paul believes there is something even better than that, however. And it is exactly the opposite of the me-monster boast.

He says, "I've been given the riches of Christ, sonship in heaven, the gift of the Holy Spirit and the promise that goodness and mercy will now follow me all the days of my life. And I deserved none of it. God gave me these things just because he loves me."

The gospel, for Paul, is the ultimate dinner-story boast.

It's the only true humble brag. And one anyone can participate in.

Paul knew that the power found in the gospel was his only hope. Paul knew he didn't have the resources to live the Christian life, much less fulfill the mission God had given him to take the gospel to the Gentiles! Paul says that in Jesus we have all the wisdom and power we need to do whatever God has called us to do. That's why he was comfortable being weak, overlooked, and despised. He was even enthusiastic about his suffering and his weaknesses if they meant being able to lean more into Christ (1 Cor. 1:20–31; Col. 1:24).

Do your insecurities and inadequacies push you deeper into gospel hope?

Or do your sufferings and weaknesses drive you farther away from the gospel?

Perhaps you know the gospel, you just don't boast in it. It's not where you turn to assure yourself the future will be okay. It's not the possession you are most excited to carry into tomorrow.

Paul says it must be if you want the joy and confidence that characterizes those who turn the world upside down!

Paul rejoices that in the gospel we have the ultimate possession (the fullness of God), have experienced the ultimate love (at the cross), have received the ultimate victory (deliverance from sin and death), and possess the ultimate assurance (Jesus now sits at the right hand of God controlling all things for my good). What more is there to boast in? Where else would we turn?

Martin Luther understood this.

## ONE LITTLE WORD

The German Protestant reformer may not have seen Jesus with his eyes like Paul did, but he did catch the same life-altering vision of the gospel. In the gospel Luther found the resources for assurance in his own relationship with God. He also found the resources to awaken an exhausted, floundering, and defeated medieval church. Luther described his discovery of the gospel like a man falling down the shaft of a bell tower and reaching out in desperation for the only rope available. As he grabbed it, he said, it not only broke his fall; it rang the bell and woke up half of Germany.

Something similar happens to all those who find the gospel.

On October 31, 2017, we celebrated the five hundredth anniversary of the beginning of the Protestant Reformation, the day Martin Luther nailed his Ninety-five Theses to the castle church door in Wittenberg. These ninety-five theses were Luther's attempt to condemn the actions of the Roman Catholic Church and explain that true salvation was found in God's forgiveness and grace offered through Jesus' sacrifice.

(I actually dressed up as the Ninety-five Theses for Halloween this past year, forever solidifying my reputation as the theological nerd in our neighborhood. But I digress.)

The whole Reformation started with a young German monk scouring the book of Romans searching for a pathway out of despair. It ended with a rediscovery of the gospel.

But Luther's discovery seemed perverse and dangerous to the religious leaders of his day. It seemed to threaten their stranglehold of power, so they made Luther appear before the authorities. They demanded that he take back what he wrote.

One of the religious leaders, Cardinal Cajetan, threatened to deport Luther to Rome to be imprisoned—and possibly burned at the stake—for the "heresy" of saying that God accepts us not because of what we have done but because of what Christ has done.

Cajetan told Luther he could walk free if he would utter just one little word: *revoco* ("I recant"). Just one little word, Cajetan said, can save you.

Luther responded that he would be the most beloved person in the empire if he would utter that word, *revoco*. But how could he deny the very understanding through which he became a Christian?

He then penned the words to the famous hymn, "A Mighty Fortress Is Our God."

> *And though this world, with devils filled / Should*
> *      threaten to undo us,*
> *We will not fear, for God has willed / His truth to*
> *      triumph through us.*
> *The prince of darkness grim / We tremble not for him;*
> *His rage we can endure / For lo! his doom is sure;*
> *One little word shall fell him.*

One little word.

The one Luther had in mind contained even more power than the one that would have gained Luther the approval of the empire:

*Credo.* I believe.

A small word that connects you to the power behind an empty tomb.

Luther knew something we often forget: *that one little word of faith accesses the very power of God.* Just saying it (from the heart), Paul claims, makes the sinner righteous (Rom. 10:9–10). Believing it sets the captive free, makes the lame walk, the blind see, and the dead live. It is, Paul said, the power of God unto salvation.

It turns tragedy into triumph.

It transforms defeated sinners into unstoppable conquerors. With the gospel no weapon formed against God's children will prosper, and all those who rise against us will fall. Confessing our belief releases in us the power of the Spirit in such a way that not even the gates of hell can resist. It is the fortress we can return to again and again. Luther's great hymn—referred to as the "Battle Cry of the Reformation"—closes with these words:

> *That word above all earthly powers / No thanks to them abideth;*
> *The Spirit and the gifts are ours / Through him who with us sideth:*
> *Let goods and kindred go / This mortal life also;*
> *The body they may kill / God's truth abideth still;*
> *His kingdom is forever!*

If we're wise, the only thing we'll boast in, hope in, and cling to is the gospel. Because in that little word—and only in that little word—is the mighty fortress of God's power.

## WASTED ENERGY

You know that Nike commercial where everyone discovers the world has stopped spinning? The news anchor confirms, "The world has stopped turning on its axis." Inspired by the sight of a nearby hamster wheel, a young woman grabs her Nikes and invites everyone she knows to run the same direction to get the world spinning again.

They start running.

Eventually, she has some notable friends join her cause—Kobe Bryant, Kevin Hart, Odell Beckham Jr., Simone Biles, even Bill Nye.

Well, they get the world spinning again. The problem is, they've been running in the wrong direction. So they all turn around and run the other way. Of course, Kevin Hart, apparently not just the comedic genius but the geophysics genius as well, knew they were going the wrong way the whole time.

I love this commercial.

But I also hate this commercial.

Hats off to Nike because the commercial did make me head down to the mall for a new pair of running shoes.

But the truth is, whether all 7.4 billion of us are running the same direction or standing on our heads doesn't affect the rotation of the earth in the slightest. You'd think that at least Bill Nye, the Pseudo-Science Guy, would have known better.

I have this same frustration with people who try to change the world through Facebook and Twitter posts. Nowhere is more energy spent with less actual output than in the machinations of social media.

I'm sure you know what I'm talking about. Those folks on Facebook who try to convince everyone that "TO NOT AGREE WITH ME ON _____ ISSUE MAKES YOU A BAD PERSON WHO HATES FREEDOM AND–OH BY THE WAY–YOU ALSO PROBABLY KICK PUPPIES AND THROW PLASTIC STRAWS IN THE INTERCOASTAL WATERWAYS!"

But are our digital rants actually changing people? Or are they more about us trying to declare our righteousness?

Reflect on your own experience. Have *you* ever changed your mind about something someone said to you in the comments of one of your Facebook posts? I've developed new opinions about the *person* doing the posting but not usually new opinions about the issue they're posting about. The longer social media exists, the more it seems to become this generation's version of shoeless, bearded men parading through downtown with sandwich boards shouting that the end of the world is at hand.

I worry that the sermons many of us hear in our churches aren't faring much better. Preaching that focuses more on changing our behavior or our opinions than changing our hearts is the same as a gloom-and-doom sandwich board. Until we experience changed hearts, all externally imposed behavioral modifications will always come up short. We'd have more luck trying to spin the earth with our running buddy Kevin Hart.

To prove this, I need to turn only to raw tomatoes and mayonnaise.

I hate tomato sandwiches. I believe God designed tomatoes to go into sauces, not onto sandwiches. (That's in the Levitical law somewhere, I think.) The only thing I hate more than tomato sandwiches? Mayonnaise.

If you like tomato and mayonnaise sandwiches, put down this book and go see a doctor. Or better yet, maybe an exorcist.

Here's the thing. If you are physically large enough, you might be able to force me to eat a tomato and mayonnaise sandwich. But that's all you're going to be able to do with that method.

Forcing me to eat one will never make me love one.

The moment you look away, I'll toss what remains.

In the same way, any external changes that don't begin with a change of heart will ultimately fade away. The end result will always be left wanting.

Sadly, a lot of a church ministry strategy uses the tomato sandwich method. These strategies get people into programs, but the programs don't bring lasting heart change. The people only act like they love whatever the program includes, when in reality all they like is getting together with the people they already know and are comfortable around.

The tomato sandwich method creates hypocrites.

And exhausted people.

And frustrated leaders.

And worst of all, a powerless church.

Pastors who are great speakers, who can bring an audience to their feet, eliciting rounds of applause and shouts of "Amen!" often fail to create the life change we see in the book of Acts. Those stories include simple people—normal, everyday folks who had been changed by the gospel's power. They were even described as not very good public speakers. Seriously, in 2 Corinthians Paul notes that his preaching had the reputation of being a big nothing-burger (10:10)!

The problem for us today is that many of our contemporary preachers are big on oratory and small on gospel. Oratory can produce emotional responses but not lasting change. As soon as the magic of the oratory is gone, so is the movement.

When the service ends, we throw away the tomato sandwich.

This is what happens when what we hear in church centers on life tips and practical wisdom. These sermons present a picture of how people ought to live, but that's the end of the road. There's no mention of the power to actually get them there. Even worse, the content of these messages (and popular books) pulls one over on the hearers/readers, mistaking their slightly improved moralistic life with the resurrected life of new creation that is characteristic of a true child of God. Efforts like these often have the look of godliness but lack the power thereof (2 Tim. 3:5).

The end result is that they only leave people confused, exhausted, and lost.

One glimpse of the glory of God, however, in the face of Jesus Christ, or one little word of faith in the finished work of Christ, can release more power into the soul of the believer than all the sermons and all the programs ever concocted in Christendom.

God, you see, is not just after obedience. He's after a *whole new kind* of obedience. God is after an obedience that grows in the soil of desire. He wants his people to be obedient because we crave righteousness, because we desire God above all else.

That kind of obedience can only be produced by the gospel.

## BORN AGAIN

Each of North America's religious awakenings has had one thing in common: a bold declaration that what God demanded from people could not be found within their own hearts. This has been the unifying theme of the preaching of Jonathan Edwards, George Whitefield, John Wesley, D. L. Moody, Billy Sunday, and Billy Graham.

Being "born again" points to something we can't do for ourselves, something that–at first–leaves us in despair. Jesus first used the phrase with a man who had every reason to think he had it all together.

The religious ruler Nicodemus said to Jesus, "we know that you are a teacher who has come from God, for no one could perform these signs you do unless God were with him" (John 3:2). Jesus, who seemed to prefer skipping small talk and flattery and cutting right to the chase, responded with, "Truly I tell you, unless someone is born again, he cannot see the kingdom of God" (v. 3).

Nicodemus was puzzled. *Born again? How can I reenter my mother's womb? Is that even physically possible?*

"Truly I tell you," Jesus responded, "unless someone is born of water and the Spirit, he cannot enter the kingdom of God" (v. 5).

"But how can one be born of the Spirit?" (You've got to hand it to Nicodemus: he's not catching a lick of what Jesus is saying, and he's still polite enough to keep asking questions.) Jesus responds,

> "As Moses lifted up the snake in the wilderness, so the Son of Man must be lifted up, so that everyone who believes in him may have eternal life. For God loved the world in this way: He gave his one and only Son, so that everyone who believes in him will not perish but have eternal life." (John 3:14–16)

Here Jesus is referring back to one of the best pictures in the Bible of what salvation looks like. It's an obscure story in the book of Numbers from the Old Testament. As a consequence of Israel's sin, God sent serpents that bit them and killed many.

Israel cried out for mercy, and God told Moses to take an image of a bronze serpent and put it up on a pole on a hilltop. If the Israelites would look upward in faith, believing that salvation and healing belonged to God, they would be healed (Num. 21:4–9).

Jesus says this is a picture of how we obtain forgiveness and spiritual healing. As we look to Jesus lifted up on the cross and say, "There is my salvation!" his righteousness is given to us. When you believe God accomplished the work of salvation, the healing power of righteousness is infused into you. That is the way you enter the Christian life. It is also the way you grow in the Christian life.

New life in you started with a look. It grows in you through a sustained look.

### Being Born Again Means Dying First

There's some bad news inherent in being born again though. To be born again, we have to acknowledge that we're currently dead. To experience the power of new birth, we have to mourn the weakness of our life without Jesus.

Nicodemus had to see that all those years of religion had not moved him one step closer to the kingdom of God (John 3:4). That was hard and humiliating for a man who had devoted his life to religious rigor, which is why so many religious people miss the gospel. But it was the only way. We have to experience the darkness of the night before appreciating the dawn. When we do, oh how glorious the morning seems!

The famous Great Awakening evangelist George Whitefield knew the power of this awakening. In his sermons Whitefield preached basically one message with two points. First, he said, we must repent of our sins. That made sense, of course. If we're going to know God, we have to stop our defiant sinning.

But second, he said, we must repent of our righteousness. This caught everyone off guard. Strengths, he said, are even more dangerous than sins because our righteousness deceives us with false confidence. We end up thinking we are sufficient in ourselves to please God. One person saved through Whitefield's preaching, a working-class man named Nathan Cole, recounted it this way: "As I heard him preach, it gave me a heart wound. By God's blessing my old foundation was broken up, and I saw that my righteousness would not save me."[2]

But before that, we have to reach that same point of despair in our own lives.

Before we can experience the power of the new birth, we have to despair the utter powerlessness of all that has come before. We have to repent of anything other than simple faith in the gospel.

But this doesn't only apply personally. Not only do we need to reach that point of despair; our churches need to reach it.

Our leaders need to reach it.

Our ministries need to reach it.

Before we soar on the heights of success, we must first understand the depths of failure that most certainly will be ours without the power of God.

## A NEW KIND OF CHRISTIAN

Without the power of the gospel, nothing will change.

If you don't believe that in theory, you will soon come to terms with it in practice.

The gospel produces a change in the church unlike anything that has come before it. Instead of proud, religious hypocrites who fear outsiders (like Paul), it creates generous, redemptive healers who attract them.

I saw this type of gospel transformation happen in our church. For years we had been a big, successful, religiously active body of Christians. It was great. We were growing. We seemed to be thriving. But something happened that completely changed the way our city perceived our presence.

You guessed it.

It was the gospel.

When the gospel really took root, our members gained the reputation for being wherever the brokenness was.

I recently had a couple tell me that when they showed up for their final interview at social services to be licensed as foster parents, they were asked why they wanted to do it. This is a common question, but they weren't sure how much to share about their religious motivations.

Sheepishly, they looked at each other and explained, "Well, we believe this is what Christ did for us when he died for our sin. He made us sons and daughters of God."

Without missing a beat, the interviewer flatly said, "You must be from The Summit Church."

"How did you know that?" they asked.

"Because everyone who comes in from The Summit Church says the same thing. We can actually track a turning point in the foster care program in Durham County from when The Summit Church got involved."

Gospel transformation.

This was right around the same time I came to the realization that the gospel was not just the baby steps of Christianity; it was the full marathon. The gospel didn't provide just some things; it provided everything—the motivation *and* the power—in the Christian life. Literally, social services in Durham could identify the time when the gospel took root in our church.

That's what will happen in our cities and our communities when the gospel roots itself deep in the soil of everything we do. When it's above all.

Don't get me wrong. I'm not saying the gospel *is* the only thing we do in the name of Jesus. I am saying the gospel *motivates* everything we do in the name of Jesus and *empowers* everything we do in the name of Jesus. When the gospel gets ahold of our hearts, we can't keep it to ourselves. We *have* to share it.

I know of a working-class couple from our church who used the profits from their wildly successful new business to purchase a couple of apartments in order to provide affordable housing for a woman in crisis and a refugee family in our area. Providing these two apartments brought them so much joy that they bought *thirty* more, hoping to do more of the same for vulnerable people in our city.

> **When the gospel gets ahold of our hearts, we can't keep it to ourselves.**

They even recruited other families from our church to live in a couple of these apartments to serve as gospel hands and feet to these marginalized groups.

Not long ago someone from the mayor's office of our city told me, "Everywhere in this city something is broken, there's someone there from The Summit Church trying to fix it. That means something to us."

It means something to me, too. It means the gospel has taken root.

I don't share these stories to draw unwarranted attention to our church. We have all kinds of problems, too. Believe me. The closer you get to us, the less impressed you'll be. As with most groups, we sound better described in books than we are experienced in person.

Our boast is the gospel.

You may not have the resources our church has. You may have more. Maybe your worship team is not as good as ours is. Maybe it is better. But our boast is not in any of these things, and yours shouldn't be either. Our boast begins in our shame. It begins in our weakness. Our boast is in the gospel. The good news is that we all have access to that same boast—every single one of us.

We all want to see our society changed. We're discouraged by the poverty, the sickness, the injustice, and the bigotry all around us. We want to make a difference. But only in the gospel are the resources found for lasting change.

We need to be active fighting injustice, providing marital help, and offering support for those trying to break free of addiction. We want to be salt and light in our community, influencing its policies for good.

But let's not think we can bring the kingdom of God with the weapons of the world—be that the sword, the dollar, or the talented musician. "If my kingdom were of this world, my servants would fight," Jesus said. "But as it is, my kingdom is not from here" (John 18:36). God's kingdom is from above, fueled by a power from above—a power that flows from a long, believing look at the finished work of Christ.

Fix your eyes on him.

Reexperience his power.

## LOOK AND LIVE

Have you ever experienced something so unbelievable, so extraordinary, that you simply couldn't stop talking about it? Biting into a perfectly cooked, Pittsburgh-style rib eye. The first time you went skydiving. The moment the Adam's Peanut Butter Fudge Ripple Cheesecake lands on your plate. Seeing *Les Misérables* on Broadway. Visiting Hawaii. Unexpectedly discovering the Nicolas Cage movie marathon on TBS.

The preaching of Charles Spurgeon drew thousands of Londoners in a time when megachurches were unheard of. Those who sat under his preaching described being gripped by a passion so real you felt like you could touch it. That passion emanated from a firsthand experience with God's power that Spurgeon simply could not shut up about. Like Luther before him (and Paul before *him*), he had been changed in an instant by a mere *look* at Jesus. In Spurgeon's story of conversion, we find a pattern for us all.

This is how he tells it. Trust me, it's worth reading at length:

> *I sometimes think I might have been in darkness and despair until now, had it not been for the goodness of God in sending a snowstorm one Sunday morning*

*while I was going to a certain place of worship. When I could go no further, I turned down a side street, and came to a little Primitive Methodist Chapel. In that chapel there may have been a dozen or fifteen people. I had heard of the Primitive Methodists, how they sang so loudly that they made people's heads ache; but that did not matter to me. I wanted to know how I might be saved, and if they could tell me that, I did not care how much they made my head ache.*

*The minister did not come that morning; he was snowed in, I suppose. At last, a very thin-looking man, a shoemaker, or tailor, or something of that sort, went up into the pulpit to preach. Now, it is well that preachers should be instructed; but this man was really stupid. He was obliged to stick to his text, for the simple reason that he had little else to say.*

*The text was, "Look unto me, and be ye saved, all the ends of the earth."*

*He did not even pronounce the words rightly, but that did not matter. There was, I thought, a glimpse of hope for me in that text. The preacher began thus—*
*"My dear friends, this is a very simple text indeed. It says, 'Look.' Now lookin' don't take a deal of pains. It ain't liftin' your foot or your finger; it is just, 'Look.' Well, a man needn't go to College to learn to look. You may be the biggest fool, and yet you can look. A man needn't be worth a thousand a year to be able to look. Anyone can look; even a child can look. But then the text says, 'Look unto Me.' Ay!" said he in broad Essex accent, "Many of you are lookin' to yourselves, but it's no use lookin' there. You'll never find any comfort in yourselves. . . . The text says, 'Look unto Me.'"*

*Then the good man followed up his text in this way:*
*"Look unto Me; I am sweatin' great drops of blood. Look unto Me; I am hangin' on the cross. Look*

*unto Me; I am dead and buried. Look unto Me; I rise again. Look unto Me; I ascend to Heaven. Look unto Me; I am sittin' at the Father's right hand. O poor sinner, look unto Me! Look unto Me!"*

*When he had gone to about that length and managed to spin out ten minutes or so, he was at the end of his tether.*

*Then he looked at me under the gallery, and I daresay, with so few present, he [must have known] I was a stranger. Fixing his eyes on me, as if he knew all my heart, he said, "Young man, you look very miserable."*

*Well, I did; but I had not been accustomed to have remarks made from the pulpit on my personal appearance. However, it was a good blow—it struck right home.*

*He continued,*

*"And you always will be miserable—miserable in life, and miserable in death—if you don't obey my text; but if you obey now, this moment, you will be saved."*

*Then, lifting up his hands, he shouted, as only a Primitive Methodist could do, "Young man, look to Jesus Christ. Look! Look! Look! You have nothin' to do but to look and live."*

*I saw at once the way of salvation. I know not what else he said—I did not take much notice of it—I was so possessed with that one thought. Like as when the brazen serpent was lifted up, the people only looked and were healed, so it was with me. I had been waiting to do fifty things, but when I heard that word, "Look!" what a charming word it seemed to me! Oh! I looked until I could almost have looked my eyes away. There and then the cloud was gone, the darkness had rolled away, and that moment I saw the sun; and I could have risen that instant, and sung with the most enthusiastic of them, of the precious blood of Christ, and the simple faith which looks alone to Him. Oh, that somebody had told me this before, "Trust Christ, and you shall be saved."*

*Yet it was, no doubt, all wisely ordered, and now I can say,—'Ever since by faith I saw the stream Thy flowing wounds supply, Redeeming love has been my theme, and shall be till I die.'"*[3]

Look and live.

That's all it takes.

With one little look, everything can change. With one little word, the powers of darkness can be disarmed. Only the gospel has this kind of power.

No wonder Spurgeon said his goal in every message was to "plow a trough back to the gospel."

> **Only the gospel, the declaration that Christ has finished the work of salvation, can produce real change.**

Only the gospel, the declaration that Christ has finished the work of salvation, can produce real change.

Only the gospel can compel persecuted churches to keep gathering, worshipping, and sharing under the threat of death or exile.

Only the gospel could turn a man who killed Christians into a man who called himself "the bondservant of Jesus Christ" and "apostle to the Gentiles."

Only the gospel could turn the morbidly introspective, legalistic monk Martin Luther into the torchbearer for the Protestant Reformation and give him the courage to hold onto the gospel even amidst threats to his life.

Only the gospel can change you. Only the gospel can change your church. Only the gospel can change your community. Only the gospel.

Not political agendas. Not programs. Not moving oratory. Not social justice initiatives. These things may flow naturally from an experience with the gospel, but they cannot replace it.

The good news is, when the gospel is above all in our churches, renewal will follow. And when renewal comes, there's just no telling what God might do next.

# CHAPTER 3

# GOSPEL
## MISSION

*"The criteria on which a church should measure its success is not how many new names are added to the roll nor how much the budget is increased, but rather how many Christians are actively winning souls and training them to win the multitudes."*
–Robert Coleman, *The Master Plan of Evangelism*

"Our biggest need right now is not more money."

I'm not sure I'd ever heard that phrase from the leader of a missions agency before, but this was what Dr. Kevin Ezell, the president of the North American Mission Board (NAMB), the largest church-planting organization in the United States, said to me and our missions pastor over dinner.

"Great," I said, "then you're picking up dinner," as I reached for the dessert menu.

"We'll always take your money, of course," he continued, "but our *greatest* need is for qualified planters. We just don't have enough qualified church planters to invest in."

NAMB is an agency of the Southern Baptist Convention, which boasts sixteen million adherents in forty-two thousand churches across the U.S.–and we have a problem finding five hundred qualified planters each year? That's only one planter for every 840 churches, or one out of every 320,000 Southern Baptist members.

Other evangelical tribes do not seem to fare much better, for what it's worth. I once heard the leader of a successful church-planting network–the one known for the lowest failure rate among their plants–explain that they were looking for ways to attract qualified planters from *outside* their network to plant churches *through* their network.

Dare we ask why one of the most effective church-planting networks has to recruit from the outside and is not raising up enough leaders from within its churches?

If we're all looking to commandeer one another's leaders, who is raising up new ones?

And if our *church plants* are not effective at raising up leaders, who is?

"The reason for this shortage, I believe," Dr. Ezell continued, "is that so few of our churches have intentional pipelines for leadership development. If we got good at disciple making again, church planting would take care of itself."

I'm beginning to think he's right.

Our failure to raise up church-planting leaders is symptomatic of our failure to raise up disciples in our churches. It seems that few of our people are engaged in, much less skilled at, making disciple-making disciples. Back in 2015, I was speaking at an event with Dr. Albert Mohler, president of the Southern Baptist Theological Seminary. Dr. Mohler said,

> The vast majority of the people who've ever been baptized by our people (the SBC) are our own offspring. We've never been very evangelistic in terms of people to whom we haven't given birth.

*We're only evangelistically effective with our own children?*
Keep in mind this is about *the Southern Baptist Convention,* the denomination in America probably most known for its evangelistic focus. (If someone shows up on your door asking if you are prepared to meet God tonight, it's most likely a Jehovah's Witness or a Southern Baptist.) And these words come not from a critical cynic, but from Albert Mohler, a beloved patriarch within the movement.

Many skills make for effective ministry. Great leadership. Great vision. Entrepreneurial grit. Disciplined execution. But all of those skills mean nothing if we aren't *making disciples,* one by one. Apart from that, all the money we raise, buildings we build, ministries we organize, sermons we preach, and songs we write don't move the mission forward. Without that mission we're wasting our time.

> **Everything we do in ministry should flow from or lead toward making disciples.**

Thus, everything we do in ministry should flow from or lead toward making disciples. Disciple making is, after all, the key component of Jesus' Great Commission (Matt. 28:19–20), and it ought to be the standard by which we judge every ministry in the church.

In his classic book *The Master Plan of Evangelism,* Robert Coleman said,

> The Great Commission is not merely to go to the ends of the earth preaching the gospel (Mark 16:15), nor to baptize a lot of converts into the name of the triune God, nor to teach them the precepts of Christ, but to "make disciples"—to build people like themselves who were so constrained by the commission of Christ that they not only followed his way but led others to as well.[1]

47

Coleman points out that in the verses that comprise the Great Commission, there is only one real imperative verb: "make disciples." Everything else from Matthew 28:19–20 that we translate into English as a verb is actually a participle. I know you're about to pull up Wikipedia right now to remember what a participle is, so let me just jump ahead to the point: it means that Jesus saw everything else he commanded in those verses—baptizing, going, teaching—as pursuant of the primary thing: disciple making.

Making disciples is the primary calling of the church.

Our mission.

Our purpose.

This means *the* criteria upon which any church should measure its success is "not how many new names are added to the roll, nor how much the budget is increased." Not even close. The success of the church is in how many Christians are actively making disciples and training them to win the multitudes.

How many of our members can look around on a Sunday morning and point to someone (outside of their family) who is there because they brought them to Christ?

How many can point to someone who is there because someone they brought to Christ brought that person to Christ?

Maybe that's not fair.

After all, we can't control how many people come to Jesus.

Okay, how many of our fellow members have been inside the home of one of their unbelieving neighbors in the last month?

If you told the people in your church to pull out their phone and text a non-Christian they were on close enough terms to that they could arrange a spontaneous coffee for later in the afternoon, how many could do it? How many of the people in your church who read their Bible daily have made an attempt to read it with an unbeliever some time in the past year?

One more: If God answered, in one fell swoop, all the prayers members in your church prayed last week, how many new people would be in the kingdom?

The uncomfortable reality is that many of the fastest growing churches in America are not growing because they are winning and discipling new believers but because they are importing them from other churches.

A familiar scenario unfolds in many of our big cities: some new hot church with great music comes into town, and everyone flocks there. That church boasts "New Testament-level" growth, but the total number of people in church in that city on any given weekend doesn't actually increase.

Of course, this isn't disciple making.

If anything, it's sheep stealing.

Swapping members is not advancing on the gates of hell; it's reshuffling soldiers into new platoons. And then hanging out in the barracks.

> **Many of the fastest growing churches in America are not growing because they are winning and discipling new believers but because they are importing them from other churches.**

For many years we wanted disciple making to be the priority in our church, but our college ministry finally led the way. Each year they launch about fifty students into ministry, most of whom come from non-Christian backgrounds. A couple of years ago they sent a full-time church-planting team to Southeast Asia that consisted of eight college graduates, *seven of whom* had become Christians at our church during their time in college. The next year fourteen interns joined our staff to help reach more college students in the area, *all fourteen of whom* had become Christians at our church during college.

What are they doing right?

They are playing on flag football teams with lost people.

They are eating meals with lost people.

They are reading the Bible with lost people.

They have taught us what the word *discipleship* means. It was simpler than we imagined. Life on life. Real friendship. Hard conversations. Intentionally missional.

As one of our college pastors says, "Seventy-five percent of all our discipleship is informal. We teach our students that almost every step of their Christian life is to be shared with someone else. When they get to whatever finish line they are headed toward, they should look around and see three or four people they have brought with them."

To reach more people, we don't need better gathering techniques; we need a more intentional focus on discipleship.

This takes an entirely new way of looking at relationships.

## BENEFIT SEEKERS OR BURDEN BEARERS?

Most of us instinctively approach every relationship with one basic question: How can this relationship help complete my life?

Can this person fill a relational need?

Can I learn something from him?

Does being with her make me happy?

But Paul says that people who understand the gospel should seek to share the burdens of others (Gal. 6:2). The person who looks out for himself, he explains, and only what he can get out of others, is blinded.

He has forgotten grace.

He has forgotten how much Jesus carried for him.

Think about the burdens that you are carrying right now. How many of them are actually the burdens of others?

Our general approach to life can be a quest to gain from others or a quest to see where we can bear the burdens of others. The gospel challenges us to lay our lives down and pour our lives out as Jesus did for us.

This is especially true in twenty-first-century North America because without this no one will ever hear our gospel.

Each year the number of those who identify as nonreligious in our society grows at an astounding rate. Pollsters call them the "nones" because they have no religious affiliation. Some cultural pundits have used those statistics to declare the end of the American church. And while this fear of secularism is a bit overblown, the stats do raise an essential point: churches that want to reach nones need to retool.

Nones will not saunter their way into church because the program is engaging, the music is cool, or the guest services are Disney-esque. Nones feel like the church is a separate world—one of which they want no part. It's less that they are disgusted at the church and more that they simply have no reason to go.

I once lived in a community that was 99.97 percent Muslim. I made up about half of that .03 percent. I was considered "unmosqued." My apartment was less than two hundred yards from a mosque. It was freshly painted with a neatly kept yard and friendly people. But at no point did I consider going.

I wouldn't have gone for a special holiday.

I wouldn't have gone if I were facing hard times.

I wouldn't have gone if the imam were doing a really helpful series on relationships or if he told really funny stories that helped me see how Allah was relevant to my life. I wouldn't have gone had they added percussion and a kickin' electric guitar to the prayer chants. Islam was a completely foreign world and one in which I knew I clearly didn't belong. So I never even considered going.

I take that back. I did visit the mosque one time because one of my Muslim friends invited me, and I wanted to honor him by learning more about his life and faith.

It didn't go well. We had to sit in uncomfortable positions for extended periods of time. And everyone but me seemed to know what to say at various points of the service. They would all suddenly stand up, in unison, leaving me clamoring to get to my feet, which was hard when you couldn't feel your legs anymore. They all dressed in the same outfit, so my Nike shirt and Levi jeans made me feel pretty out of place.

At the end of one of the prayers, they all in unison sang out, "Amen." At that point I thought I knew the drill, hearkening back to my days in a country Baptist church. So I hit the harmony note. No one else deviated from the melody line.

I slipped out during the final announcements.

My friend invited me back several times, but I always managed to find a reason to not be able to go. The mosque was a portal to a completely different world—one I had no reason or desire to enter.

This is a bit what it is like for people in the post-Christian West as they look into the Christian church. A British friend of mine, Steve Timmis, cites a study in Great Britain in which 70 percent of Brits say they have no intention of ever attending a church service. For any reason.

Not at Easter.

Not for marriages.

Not for funerals or Christmas Eve services.

Seventy percent! Great Britain may be a few years ahead of the United States in the progress of secularization, but judging by the rapidly increasing presence of the nonreligious, this is where we are headed, too.

That means that each year the number of people in our communities who might wander into our churches without an invitation is shrinking. If we don't equip our people to carry the gospel outside of our churches, we will lose all contact with the unreached people living around us. Without a new strategy the future looks like a few flashy megachurches fighting with one another for larger pieces of a rapidly shrinking pie.

Somebody needs to grow the pie!

If we are going to move the mission needle in the United States, we need an intentional process to turn unbelievers into church leaders, atheists into missionaries.

*We need to get better at making disciples.*

## NOT AS HARD AS YOU THINK

Being a Christian means everything in your life changes, but living as a Christian doesn't mean you change everything about your life.

That sound confusing?

During the course of a day, Christians still do most of the things they did before they became Christians.

Hear me out.

Being a Christian doesn't mean you stop eating, going to work, taking trips, shopping for groceries, dropping your clothes off at the dry cleaners, reading good books, watching great movies, or spending time with your family.

Christians still wash their clothes.

Christians still eat food.

Christians still watch basketball.

Sure, Christians enter some of these things differently. But in general, living as a disciple maker means opening your life up to do those things with lost people. We still do all the things normal people do, just under the banner of the Great Commission.

Discipleship simply means doing the everyday stuff of your life with other people while walking toward Jesus, step-by-step, day by day, meal by meal, conversation by conversation.

If you think about it like that, making disciples is fairly simple—you just bring people along in your spiritual journey. Discipleship is more about opening up your life than walking someone through a program. If you have Christian habits in your life worth imitating, you can be a disciple maker. It doesn't require years of training; you just teach others to follow Christ as you follow him (1 Cor. 11:1).

Rosaria Butterfield, whom I'll introduce to you more properly in chapter 6, says that the home is the most important evangelistic instrument in the believers' tool kit, especially if our goal is to reach people far from God. The home is where unbelievers can feel the warmth of God's acceptance. The home is where they can see our way of life up close enough to ask a reason for the hope that enlivens us. The home is where we turn "strangers into neighbors and neighbors into family."

Rosaria points out that the vast majority of Jesus' personal encounters with lost people happened over meals in homes. In fact, she says, in the Gospels, Jesus seems to be always coming from a meal, at one, or on his way to one. He pretty much eats his way through the Gospel of Luke.

That's a Savior I can get excited about following.

This is how we will most effectively reach people with the gospel today.

Technically, the Great Commission says, "As you are going, make disciples." In other words, Jesus assumed that life itself would provide the context for disciple making.

## READ THE BIBLE AS YOU GO

I asked one of the most effective disciple makers I know to share with me his discipleship method. I was expecting a fancy curriculum with a silver-bullet technique. Instead, he sent me a scanned list of thirty-one Bible verse references he had typed out on a word processor back in the '80s. He told me that he gives this list to someone and asks them to take one verse a day and write beside each of the references what God might be saying to them through it. He meets with them weekly to discuss their answers. After that, he said, he asks them if they want to read a book of the Bible together and do the same thing.

That was it.

No secret sauce, no electrifying jolt of discipleship genius, no magic formula, no Jedi mind tricks. Yet just about every time our churches had a baptism service, that disciple maker had somebody represented in the lineup—either from him directly or through someone he'd led to Christ bringing someone else to Christ. Just last weekend I met a guy who had been led to Christ by a guy who had been led to Christ by a guy who had been led to Christ by a guy who had been led to Christ by a guy who had been led to Christ by a guy who had been led to

Christ by this guy. If you are counting, that's six generations. That means he is a spiritual great-great-great-great-grandfather, and he's not even fifty years old yet!

Oh yeah, he's not seminary trained.

What about you?

As you go through the normal rhythms of life, invite someone to travel alongside you and read the Bible together along the way. Let the pressures of life, God's Word, and the Holy Spirit carry the heavy load. You'll be amazed at the results.

You may be good at many dimensions of the Christian life, but are you good at making disciples? Can you point to others serving in the mission now who were not believers when you met them? Are you reproducing yourself?

What a tragedy if we spend our whole life busy doing good things but overlook the *one* thing Jesus told us was paramount, the one thing he identified as *the Great Commission*!

## THE NUMBERS DON'T LIE

How great would it be if you were a major league baseball scout for the Boston Red Sox?

One of my good friends, Mike, is.

When people find that out, he suddenly becomes the most interesting man in the world. Turns out just about everyone knows someone (or *is* someone) who could have gone pro if only they'd been given a look.

Once when we were eating lunch, a waiter asked if we could meet him after our meal to toss the ball around. He wanted to see if Mike thought he was worth a shot in training camp. Mike actually did it. I told him that if this turned out to be one of those storybook moments of discovery where this overlooked waiter becomes the greatest pitcher of all time, when they made the movie later I wanted my character to be played by Nicolas Cage.

Come to think of it, I should have gotten that in writing.

Mike has scouted for the Red Sox for more than a decade as they've gone from being the team under the "curse of the Bambino" to winner of four of the last fifteen World Series. He tells me that scouting is altogether different than it used to be. It's less about having naked instinct for talent and more about advanced statistical analysis. The same is true in other sports as well. Twenty years ago an NBA scout would assess players based on height, points, rebounds, assists per game, and the "feel" the scout got from watching them. Today it's about "player efficiency rating" and points or rebounds per minute.

Why? Because we have more accurate numbers than ever, and numbers don't lie.

The same is true when it comes to our churches and our denominations. Our conferences and worship services may *feel* better than ever, but the numbers don't lie.

Baptisms and church membership in evangelical churches continue to decrease year over year.

In the Southern Baptist Convention alone, church membership decreased by more than two hundred thousand from 2016 to 2017, and the number of baptisms dropped by almost 10 percent.

The ratio of total church members of Southern Baptist churches to baptisms is an abysmal 59:1.

Think about that.

For almost every sixty members of the United States' largest Protestant denomination, there is only one new baptism a year. Does it really take sixty of us to lead *one* person to Christ?

Christians across the denominational board just aren't sharing their faith and making disciples. In one LifeWay study among North American Protestants, 78 percent of churchgoers said they had shared their faith with exactly zero people in the last six months.[2]

Zero.

*In six months.*

It's hard for me to think of a topic I care anything at all about that I *haven't* talked about in six months–whether my passion for it is positive or negative.

Outback's bloomin' onion–positive.

The appropriate use of the Oxford comma–positive.

Nic Cage movies–hard to describe how positive.

My increasing inability to read small font–negative.

Fear that I'll get E. coli from an unwashed apple–negative.

Duke basketball–the worst.

I can't think of anything I care about that hasn't come up in conversation in six months.

And yet that's where most of our people are when it comes to sharing their faith. They believe the gospel is the power for salvation. They believe they should be sharing that gospel with others. But it's just not happening. What's going on?

Changes in how we play church aren't going to matter at all if we don't address the core problem: we're not making disciples who make disciples. Our churches have seen a seeker-sensitive revolution, innovations in guest services, advances in technology, and great improvement in our worship experiences. But take a look at the "disciple-making" dial, and it seems frozen.

Sermons, books, and podcasts are great, but certain dimensions of discipleship can only happen in the context of relationships. Disciples are formed by disciple makers–intentionally, personally, one soul at a time.

There's just no shortcut.

### Lack of Strategy

Tragically, most churches don't even have an explicit strategy for addressing this. At our church we have adopted the phrase, "We exist to create a movement of disciple-making disciples in RDU (our city area) and around the world." We have put forward "plumb lines" which we repeat *ad nauseam*, like, "Every member is a missionary" and "We measure our success by sending capacity, not seating capacity." We say that the best ministry ideas are in the congregation, and we end every service with, "You are sent." We are trying to ingrain into every member of The Summit Church the truth that the Great Commission belongs *to them*. It takes time, repetition, and intentionality to create a culture, but it's one we desperately want to create.

It's the culture that spawned the greatest missional advance in history.

The gospel didn't advance in the early church through professional Christians and expert pastors; the gospel spread by the power of God working in and through the lives of normal people. Gospel advancement happens when ordinary people are empowered by the Spirit of God and march forward into the world demonstrating the generosity of Jesus, the forgiveness available through his cross, and the eternal hope of his coming kingdom.

> **Gospel advancement happens when ordinary people are empowered by the Spirit of God.**

Does your church have a clearly outlined path for raising up disciple-making disciples?

In the church I grew up in, we went out soul-winning every Wednesday afternoon. I got saved on a Friday and went out on my first soul-winning cold call that next Wednesday. It was my first act of sanctification! Because of that practice, within my first two years of being a Christian, I had shared the gospel dozens, if not hundreds, of times.

Most churches have moved away from this cold-call methodology, and perhaps for good reason. *The problem is, we haven't replaced it with anything.* How are people in your church learning to share the gospel, and how are they getting experience in doing so?

When it is "prayer request" time, are a significant number of the requests about people who don't yet know Christ that people in your small group are sharing the gospel with? Or are they about Great-Aunt Ruth, who is having a strange growth removed from her back next Tuesday? We sometimes referred to our Wednesday night prayer meeting as an "organ recital," where we got all kinds of updates on church members' relatives' organs. What if, instead of organ recitals, we prayed in boldness and faith with our friends, neighbors, and loved ones who don't yet know Jesus?

Again: *If God, in one fell swoop, answered all the prayers members in your church prayed last week, how many new people would be in the kingdom?*

### Lack of Belief

Maybe it's not lack of strategy.

Maybe it's more basic than that.

Maybe it's just good, old-fashioned unbelief.

I believe many Christians do not share the gospel because they are not convinced, in their hearts, that people *actually* go to hell.

The creed they endorse may claim that, but functionally they are universalists. In their hearts they assume that God grades on a curve, and most good, sincere folks out there of whatever religion will eventually make it.

God *is* a God of love, right?

Can I be candid for a moment? I struggle with this, too. In fact, I never realized how deep-seated my own lack of true belief was until I met Rhonda.

Rhonda was in her mid-twenties and had grown up in New England, far from my Bible Belt background. It's rare, even today, to find an American who has never heard anything about Christianity. But that was Rhonda.

So I started with the basics—who God is, why Jesus came, and how we could receive him as Lord and Savior. She asked lots of questions. But I wasn't prepared for the question she asked last.

"You actually believe this?"

"Yes, of course I do," I said.

She replied, "Because you don't act like you believe it. If I believed what you are saying—that everyone in my life who didn't know Jesus was separated from God's love and headed to hell—I'm not sure how I would make it through the day. I would constantly be on my knees pleading with people to listen."

She kept going.

"You don't seem that bothered by all this. You lay out the details pretty well, but it seems like a philosophical question, not what you say it is—a matter of life and death."

I felt like I had been punched in the gut. I knew she was right.

If we really believe what the Bible says about the gospel—both the good news and the bad news that precedes the good news—how can our hearts remain unengaged? Charles Spurgeon was once asked by a student whether those who had never heard about Jesus could be saved.

"A troubling question indeed," he said. "But even more troubling was whether we who knew the gospel and were doing nothing to bring it to the lost could be saved."

Mic drop.

The friend I referred to above, whom I described as one of the most effective disciple makers I've ever met, says that effective evangelism comes not from having the right personality type or adopting the right program but from two convictions:

**Conviction 1:** Salvation belongs to God.

**Conviction 2:** Faith comes only by hearing.

Believing the first releases you from the burden of feeling like it's all on you, like you have to say just the right things in just the right ways at just the right times in order to produce faith in someone's heart. God does that. That's liberating.

But believing the second premise makes you realize that God has chosen to use *us* to bring people to Jesus through our gospel witness. There is no other way, no plan B. In the book of Acts, the gospel is proclaimed only from human mouths. God produces faith in people's hearts, but he only does that through the Word we sow into them. That's motivating.

You show me someone who believes both—truly believes both—and I'll show you someone who has probably shared Christ with his neighbor.

## MAKING A GOSPEL DENT IN A DISTRACTED AGE

Here's an insight never included in the *How to Grow a Megachurch Handbook*:

> *Jesus' vision for the rapid expansion of the church did not center around hyper-talented communicators gathering large groups of people who sit in awe of their teaching methods but ordinary members raised up and sent out in the power of the Spirit.*

Ordinary people with the gospel on their lips and Spirit in their hearts would most effectively catalyze the disciple-making-disciple movement in every highway and hedge of every nation on earth.

Let me take a brief break from talking about Nicolas Cage—the greatest actor of our generation—to talk about a distant runner-up, Tom Cruise.

I promise this connects.

Tom Cruise is famous for pulling off his own stunts in his nonstop, high-octane action sequences, to the level of even injuring himself in the process. However, in the latest installment of his *Mission: Impossible* franchise (I think it was MI: 403), Cruise became the first actor to perform a HALO jump on camera.

A HALO jump is a high-altitude, low-open sky dive where the diver opens his parachute at a low altitude after a free fall for an extended period of time. In the military the HALO technique can be used to deliver equipment or supplies over enemy territory without being detected. Thus, the method protects the cargo, the crew, and the aircraft. As you might imagine, it's incredibly risky.

Tom Cruise actually did this. He did this even after breaking an ankle earlier in the film's production. And he did it *several times*. Cruise and his team did 106 jumps to capture the three scenes for the final sequence that made it into the film.

That's impressive stuff. But here's the thing: *Evangelism isn't a HALO jump.*

Evangelism is best done not as sneaky little attacks into unfamiliar territories but in the context of normal life relationships.

Rosaria Butterfield says, "Stop thinking of witnessing to your neighbors as sneaky evangelistic raids into their sinful lives."[3] Evangelism is best done as the verbal witness we offer in the context of a life we've lived in front of them.

How we conduct our families, engage in business, live in our neighborhoods, and embrace our communities *enhances* the message. In the context of normal life, we can match the strength of our words with the strength of a relationship—which is absolutely critical in a post-Christian age.

Our lives matter.

We aren't Mr. Cruise, trying to get in, drop off a package, and get out.

Tim Keller compares this to finding out the new pastor at your church—who can preach incredibly winsome sermons—is abusive toward his wife and dishonest in his business practices. Suddenly his sermons lose their appeal. And the flip is true also. You are much more likely to trust a pastor whose oratory skills are mediocre if you've seen his consistency of life and experienced his genuine compassion in your own moments of pain.

*In an age of skepticism, relational connection is crucial for overcoming barriers to belief.*[4]

This is all the more crucial because our culture suffers from another ailment perhaps even more deadly than disbelief.

Distraction.

Go ahead—check your phone and see if any of your friends have posted something new on Instagram in the 8.4 seconds since you checked it last.

Professor Alan Noble makes the case that in our age of hyper-distraction, only a disruptive witness will get someone's attention. "I believe the convergence of two major trends in our own time," he says, "calls for a new assessment of the barriers to faith." These two major trends, he says, are:

1. The endless barrage of stimulus from smartphones, Netflix, creature comforts, and thrill rides that offer instant gratification and discourage reflection and meditation.

2. The growth of secularism, in which theism is seen as one of many viable choices for human satisfaction, but in which true connection with God feels less and less plausible.[5]

The result of these trends is that when we speak of Christianity, we cannot assume our hearers understand the faith as anything other than another option in the personal-fulfillment smorgasbord. Sociologists say we "read" more words than ever before, but we don't actually read. We skim. We surf. Nothing ever really goes deep.[6] In such a world the work of witnessing and defending the faith must involve rethinking how we communicate.[7]

In other words, there's a reason our door-to-door evangelism tactics aren't seeing as much fruit.

Picture an evangelistic encounter in, say, Texas, in 1970. "If you died tonight," the earnest evangelist might ask, "where would you spend eternity?" (We always thought people died at night in those days. No one asked why.)

But even that seemingly simple question is based on many shared assumptions. Your hearer must assume that there is an afterlife and that not everyone will end up in the same place.

He must believe that there is some standard, some criteria that determine where we will end up.

In those days, even if the hearer did not believe in Jesus, he at least knew the terms. Christianity was once the basic lens through which Western society saw the world. But today it's just one of many options.

Not only that, but 1970 was a quiet enough era—before cell phones, laptops, tablets, Netflix, Snapchat, or Instagram—that we could assume our hearers would have the time and the mental space to reflect on such questions. Today we have a culture designed to keep us from reflecting at all. While you're at the front door asking about eternal destinies, Netflix is on pause waiting to resume. And after they finish the episode they're on, Netflix will automatically roll to the next one. If they get bored with this show, there are another five in the queue ready to occupy them until (or past) bedtime—or they can just hop back on social media while the not-quite-satisfying seventh episode is still rolling. Some headline is always breaking. Somebody, somewhere, just said something outrageous that demands our immediate attention. Or they can just catch up on those vacation pictures posted by their best friend's son's girlfriend's veterinarian's stepdaughter.

Even if you had a really good conversation on the porch, they likely spent little time actually thinking about and wrestling with what you said.

We have a society seemingly designed to eliminate space for reflection.

In the car ride to work tomorrow, we have satellite radio, talk radio, and podcasts to fill the void. If we take a walk in the evening, we'll likely play an audiobook on our phones. While we fix dinner, we will ask Alexa to catch us up on the evening news. Or tell us the weirdest headlines of the day. At my local mall, music and advertisements emanate from speakers in the flowerbeds so that not even that ten-second walk between Apple and Barnes & Noble is spent in silence!

And don't forget the supercomputer you carry around in your pocket. The one that buzzed six times since you started this chapter. That small device connects us to two billion people around the world through just one app alone—Facebook.

No wonder we're distracted.

The point is, there's just not a lot of space for meditation and reflection throughout our day. And that poses a significant challenge to gospel conversations.

The seventeenth-century French philosopher Blaise Pascal could not have imagined the world of distraction we live in today. And yet even he recognized the human heart's tendency to avoid the weightiest questions in life. He said that life is like a giant party, full of happy people, loud music, and dancing. But in the midst of this party, at random intervals, a monster bursts through the doors, grabbing a random partygoer and tearing him to pieces in front of everyone's eyes. This monster would then drag the bloody corpse from the room. This happens at regular enough intervals for people to realize that soon enough the monster is coming for everyone. When it happens, everyone watches in horror, only to go back to the frivolity as soon as the monster leaves.

That monster is our impending death. And it's coming for all of us.

Pascal found it absurd to live without contemplating death. We, the human race, don't like thinking about how short life is. Distraction is our preferred coping method. Our society has elevated the art of distraction to epic levels. But it doesn't matter—Pascal's monster is still on the hunt and ravaging people all around us.

All the while, we've glued our eyes to the small glowing rectangles in our pockets.

Better preaching isn't going to cut it to overcome these barriers.

Only one thing can:

*Presence.*

We can only overcome the unique barriers of our modern age by being involved enough in someone's life—at the expense of crowding our dinner table and our daily schedules—so that we can speak the right words in the right moments. God still creates circumstances that cause people to ask eternal questions. But if we are not there in relationship with them when those things happen, they will likely get distracted and turn to something else before seeking out the answer.

God was and is present among us. So too must we be with one another.

This is why ordinary people committed to becoming disciple-making disciples is God's only plan for a future of the church in America—for the church everywhere, for that matter. Let me suggest three simple commitments that, if we make them, I believe will lead to us make a gospel dent in a distracted age.

### 1. We Must Know the Gospel

It sounds obvious, but we have to know the gospel to share it well. Author and pastor Jeff Vanderstelt explains that to share the gospel well we must be as fluent in the gospel as we are with any other language. The vast majority of Christians aren't. Sure, they can bang out a few clunky phrases but not with the precision of articulation and tone that comes from fluency.

When you ask the average churchgoer what the gospel is, you get a sloppy amalgamation of spiritual jargon, moral concepts, and spiritual disciplines.

We have to become fluent in the gospel. We have to get it right, and we have to know how to share it with skill and precision.

Why? Because a false gospel can't save anyone. If the gospel is the power of God for salvation, then getting it wrong keeps people from its power.

Peter told the Jewish rulers that he could not be quiet about Jesus because there was "no other name under heaven given to people by which we must be saved" (Acts 4:12). Jesus told

Thomas, "I am *the way,* the truth, and the life. No one comes to the Father except through me" (John 14:6).

There is no other power.

There is no other name.

There is no other way.

Only Jesus.

I once heard the tragic story of a few high school kids that decided, in an ill-conceived prank, to paint over the lines on a rural mountain road. The result was as predictable as it was horrific. One night, when visibility was poor, a bus missed a curve and plunged over the side of the road, killing everyone inside. We hear a story like that and think, *Why would anyone do something so foolish and dangerous?*

But can't we be guilty of doing the same thing?

We have to keep the boundary lines of heaven clear.

We have to get the gospel right.

### 2. We Must Know Our Context

The second commitment we must make for effective evangelism is to know our context. Alan Noble is right that we're living in a different world from thirty, fifty, or a hundred years ago. Shoot, with technology as it is, we're almost living in a different world every *ten* years!

I upgraded my computer recently—same brand and model as before, only the newer version—and now my old power plugs don't work anymore. Really? I had to buy all new power cords. What's happening? The toaster oven has literally kept the same power plug technology since it was invented in 1893. Why can't my computer?

But a changing society means the questions people are asking are different, as are the ways they hear, communicate, and express truth. Our gospel remains the same, but how we deliver it does not.

In seminary my international missions professor explained that the job of the missionary is to extract the eternal water of life out of the cup of our culture and put it into the cup of the culture we are trying to reach. This is a process theologians call "contextualization," and it can be tricky. On the one hand, we don't want to water down or change the truth. Lose the truth and you'll lose the power of God on the other side of it. On the other, we don't want to present our cultural preferences as if they were divine dictates, spiritual standards for all people at all times. Paul's strongest words in his epistles were for those who presented their cultural traditions as essential gospel doctrines.

International missionaries have been having this conversation for years. Many of us in the North American context need to start having it too.

We will explore the ins and outs of this in chapter 8. For now, suffice it to say that there is no escaping contextualization. We're all doing it, even if we don't know we are.

I grew up hearing certain pastors rail against compromising gospel integrity with these "new techniques" and ungodly cultural compromises, all the while preaching from a wooden pulpit wearing a three-piece suit after singing with the accompaniment of a pipe organ.

Were any of those things present in the first century when Jesus launched the church? These elements of the church service are just as contextualized, only to a different culture.

But the gospel didn't *first* come to us from a pulpit in Alabama in 1970. It first came to us from the Middle East two thousand years ago, and faithful missionaries have sought to contextualize it to the cultures they were sent into ever since.

Changing our styles, our systems, and our services to reach new generations or new cultures is hard, but it gets easier when you really love the people you are trying to reach. When you really love someone, you'll want to remove any unnecessary obstacles keeping them from coming to Jesus.

I'm getting ahead of myself. Again, more on this in chapter 8.

A marriage counselor once told me that if I wanted to be a good husband I should become a fervent, devoted, lifelong student of two things: the Bible and my wife. It was not enough to know what the Bible teaches on marriage. I had to know her as well—to know what motivates, pleases, assures, and comforts her.

The same is true in evangelism. We can't *just* love our Bibles; we have to love lost people as well. Enough to "study" them. Enough to be willing to do what it takes to reach them.

### 3. We Must Know the Urgency

We've already mentioned Nike once. But the famous Nike slogan is a good one to remember here.

*Just do it.*

It's a helpful phrase to call to mind when you're looking for motivation to get up and go work out. Stop making excuses. Stop waiting on the right moment. Just do it.

Nike's slogan is also a great motto for how we should think about evangelism. Sure, we all have the excuses:

*I don't have the spiritual gift of evangelism.* Yeah, but a spiritual gift is (usually) just a special empowerment for a duty given to all Christians. Some people, for example, have the gift of faith. That means that they have a special ability to perceive what God wants to do in a moment and trust him to do it. That doesn't mean people without that gift don't need to show faith. The same is true with the gift of generosity. Some people have it, possessing the supernatural ability to give in just the right times and just the right ways. That doesn't mean that all Christians don't have the duty to be generous. The same is true of evangelism.

*I'll feel awkward.* Of course you will. My favorite definition of *evangelism* is "two very nervous people talking to each other." But don't you think someone's soul is worth the risk of a little awkwardness?

*I'll probably say the wrong thing.* Yep, you probably will. But God once used a donkey to speak to man, so there's hope for you. And me, too.

*I won't say the wrong thing—I'll just sit there in stupefied silence.* You'll be surprised how the Holy Spirit guides you when you put yourself out there. He'll prompt you with questions and insights. But here's the thing: *you don't get that insight until you make the leap to start the conversation.* I call it the "Michael Jordan philosophy of witnessing." (Trademark pending.) The Air Man himself was once asked if he visualized all the crazy, acrobatic moves he would perform when dunking before he started driving the lane.

"No," he said, "I just jump and decide in the air."

Take the jump, and the Holy Spirit will take over. It has happened to me literally hundreds of times.

*They'll ask a question I can't answer.* They probably will. It still happens to me. Good news—even the apostles found themselves unable to answer certain questions. Read the story of Peter and John defending themselves before the Sanhedrin in Acts 4:1–22. After listening to them explain themselves, they assumed they were "ignorant and unlearned men." The great news is that you don't have to have all the answers to faithfully deliver the message with power. The apostles never compelled people to follow Jesus because they could answer every question. They compelled them to follow Jesus *because he rose from the dead.* We're not philosophers charged to explain life's mysteries but witnesses commissioned to point to an empty tomb. Faith, I've heard it said, happens when the unexplainable meets the undeniable. We are sent out as witnesses of the undeniable resurrection.

*I might alienate my friend.* Yes, you might. But do you care enough for your friend to risk losing the relationship if it means the potential of saving that soul?

The atheist and Las Vegas magician Penn Jillette said in a viral YouTube video[8] that he didn't understand why his atheist friends got mad at Christians who shared Christ with them.

"I get mad when they *don't*," he said. "How badly do you have to hate someone to believe what you believe about Jesus and *not tell them?*"

All of these things and even more will happen over the course of a life of sharing the gospel. But we cannot be deterred.

The apostle Paul wrote in 2 Corinthians 4:7, "Now we have this treasure in clay jars, so that this extraordinary power may be from God and not from us."

Do you feel like a dumpy old clay jar? That's okay. Jars aren't valuable because of what they're made of but because of what they contain.[9]

We may be unimpressive. We might crack under pressure. But this is on purpose. The very point of God using weak messengers like us is to put his glory on display, not ours.

Some of my most powerful evangelism encounters have come when I really felt like I botched the job. On the other hand, some of the sermons I felt like I absolutely nailed saw little fruit. Other times still, I feel like the message I gave was so bad that I might be in danger of having my calling revoked, and yet inevitably those are the messages someone tells me how it changed their life.

I don't think this is accidental. I think it's just God's sense of humor. He sometimes orchestrates it this way to remind me I'm just a clumsy jug of mud.

So don't worry, friend. You will mess up. You will make things awkward. You'll probably even experience some relational tension along the way.

We all do.

But producing flawless, clean conversion stories is not your job.

That's God's. Salvation belongs to him.

You just be faithful and share the gospel. Because faith comes only by hearing.

That's your part.

Just do it!

## WHO'S YOUR ONE?

In 1954, the Southern Baptist Convention set a goal of getting one million people in Sunday school. If you don't know what Sunday school is, well, ask your parents.

They called the campaign "Million More in '54." It was a crazy big goal, and even though they didn't reach a million, they were able to get six hundred thousand more people baptized and engaged in church that year. Many of those people trusted Christ for the first time.

That's what happens when you put forward a vision of what's possible.

Recently at The Summit Church, we tried something similar.

We asked each member of our congregation to identify one person they could pray for and seek to bring to Christ over the year.

*Just one.*

The phrase we kept repeating was, "Who's your one?"

It's not an elaborate or complicated idea. Start praying for one person you can befriend, invite to church, and share Christ with. Or make a commitment that you'll have at least one unbeliever in your home for a meal at least once a month.

Don't count your kids in that.

This simple idea led to the most evangelistically effective year in our church's history. We ended up baptizing seven hundred people that year. It was amazing to see our people stand in the baptistery with a new believer and tell me later, "That was her! She was my one!"

Best prayer request I've ever gotten from a member: "Pastor, we just baptized my *one*! Will you pray for me that God gives me a new *one*?"

What if every Christian committed to praying specifically and fervently for one person, aiming to share Christ with them in intentional ways this next year?

What if just the *pastors* did it?

The impact would be staggering.

So, who's *YOUR* one?

Are you willing to ask God right now to reveal one to you?

# CHAPTER 4

# **GOSPEL**
# MULTIPLICATION

*"Making disciples . . . is messy. It is slow, tedious, even painful at times. It is all these things because it is relational. Jesus has not given us an effortless step-by-step formula for impacting nations for his glory. He has given us people, and he has said, 'Live for them. Love them, serve them, and lead them. Lead them to follow me, and lead them to lead others to follow me. In the process you will multiply the gospel to the ends of the earth.'"*
–David Platt, *Radical*

They say that the recurring dream some people have of showing up somewhere with no clothes on reveals a subconscious insecurity about your personal deficiencies. I have that feeling many Sundays when I stand up to preach because Raleigh-Durham is home to the highest concentration of PhDs in the nation, and I know that many of the people in the audience are much, much smarter than I am.

Take, for instance, a young lady I recently met who is a nurse on the cardiac wing at Duke Hospital. She moved to Durham from her home in Indiana where she went to college and graduated valedictorian of her class. Recently I learned that she had won her middle school regional spelling bee. And in the state spelling bee, she came in second place.

Of course, when I heard this, I thought the same thing you are thinking right now.

*What was the word that secured for her the regional title?*

Czechlosovakia.

Wait a minute. That's not right.

C-z-e-c-h-o-s-l-o-v-a-k-i-a.

There you have it.

And the word that put her out at states, garnering for her that disappointing second place?

Potato.

Apparently, she put that sneaky "e" on the end that's only there when potato is plural. (I told her not to feel bad. She's too young to remember, but Vice President Dan Quayle did the same thing.)

I grew up thinking that if God wanted you to be a missionary, he would spell it out in your Cheerios. I thought it would probably happen like this: as I was enjoying a heart-healthy breakfast in the morning, the Os in my bowl would mysteriously form into the word *Mumbai*.

Or something like that.

And maybe if it was a really detailed word from the Lord, I thought I should heat up a bowl of alphabet soup. Alas, I stared at my Cheerios for years, and they never spelled Mumbai or Paris or Guatemala or Czechoslovakia.

All I ever got was, "Oooooooooooooo."

But the call to missions, I discovered later, was typically not a mysterious, spine-tingling encounter. In fact, the call to leverage your life for the Great Commission was *included* in the call to follow Jesus that every Christian receives. "'Follow me,' Jesus told them, 'and I will make you fish for people'"

(Mark 1:17). If you are following Jesus, he intends to use you to "fish for people."

Every Christian is responsible to leverage his or her life for the sake of others. Jesus calls us to live in such a way that our lives mirror his, and through that reflection the world grabs on, and Jesus reels them back in to himself.

Friend, here is a world-rocking truth:

If you are a Christian, you are called.

That's right. You are called.

You.

Stop looking around. *You.*

And no, you don't need to go grab a bowl of Cheerios to seek confirmation. You don't even need to wait on a still, small voice.

Who needs a still, small voice when you have a plainly written verse?

> **Every Christian is responsible to leverage his or her life for the sake of others.**

> As he was walking along the Sea of Galilee, he saw two brothers, Simon (who is called Peter), and his brother Andrew. They were casting a net into the sea—for they were fishermen. "Follow me," he told them, "and I will make you fish for people." Immediately they left their nets and followed him. (Matt. 4:18–20)

Jesus had barely begun his public ministry, and he already had his eye on his succession plan. Jesus' plan for world evangelization can be summarized in one word

*Multiplication.*

## GREATER WORKS THAN JESUS?

From the beginning of his ministry, Jesus' plan was to leave a force on earth greater than himself. I know something sounds off about that. After all, no one is greater than Jesus, right? (Right. That's not a trick question.) But Jesus' words in John 14:12 lay it out for us: "Truly, truly, I say to you, whoever believes in me will also do the works that I do; and greater works than these will he do, because I am going to the Father" (ESV).

Greater works than *Jesus?*

I'm glad Jesus said that, not me. That's the kind of boast that gets you labeled a heretic. Have any of us ever healed the sick with greater power, or prayed with greater passion, than Jesus?

But if Jesus said it, we've got to take it seriously. Theologians say that our works can legitimately be called "greater than Jesus'" in at least two ways.

### From Death to Life

Although Jesus' earthly miracles illustrated his power to save from sin, the greatest miracle of all is conversion from death to life, which happens every time someone believes the gospel we are preaching.

Jesus fed five thousand to show he was the all-satisfying bread of life.

Jesus walked on water to show he was sovereign over everything in the believer's life.

But when I preach the gospel each weekend, people are released from eternal condemnation, reunited with God, and guaranteed eternal life.

Nik Ripken tells of Russian believers who are currently seeing miraculous signs that would rival anything in the book of Acts. Blind people receiving their sight, paralyzed people walking again. Seriously, mind-blowing stuff. But these believers only use the word *miracle* to refer to conversion. Why? Because amazing acts of deliverance pale in comparison to what God does when he draws someone to himself.

When we preach the gospel and sinners believe, *we are doing the greater work*. Jesus' miracles, according to him, were only signs. We get to preach about the thing those signs pointed to!

### Fishing in More Than One Place

The second way our works are "greater" than Jesus' is in their range. When Jesus was on earth, the Holy Spirit was "contained," so to speak, in one place and on one person. Jesus could do a lot—quite a bit more than any single one of us—but he couldn't be in two places at once.

But the Spirit can.

Through the Holy Spirit, God is in every believer, and the collective impact, Jesus says, of the Spirit multiplied in millions of believers is greater than if even he himself stayed to lead the fishing trips.

Jesus didn't have to do it this way, of course. He could have built a big congregation by choosing a good location, preaching there consistently, and doing miracles—pretty much forever. I'm sure he wouldn't have had an issue raising enough money for a permanent facility. He would've been able to draw crowds whenever he wanted.

Even without smoke.

Or moving lights.

Or a drum loop.

Or even a T-shirt cannon.

He could have commissioned a group of hyper-anointed orators who could gather throngs of people with the eloquence of their words.

But that wasn't his strategy.

Instead, he left a group of ordinary, mostly blue-collar workers with the power of the Spirit and the promise that whomever they brought to faith in Christ would receive that power also. In fact, the masses abandoned Jesus by the time he went to the cross, and instead of chasing them down to build up his following, he kept his focus on the team of twelve he'd first assembled in Matthew 4.

Jesus spent the only three years of his public ministry pouring into these twelve, teaching them about God and the kingdom, preparing them for life after he would return to heaven, and modeling for them how to make disciples. As Paul would later state it to Timothy, Jesus poured himself into faithful followers who would later do the same also:

> What you have heard from me in the presence
> of many witnesses, commit to faithful men who
> will be able to teach others also. (2 Tim. 2:2)

We see four generations of people in that one sentence: Paul, Timothy, faithful men, and others also. Implied is the person who poured into Paul, Ananias, and the one who poured into *him*, Peter, and the one who poured into Peter (guess who?), Jesus. Ultimately, all of us can trace our spiritual lineage, person by person, back to Jesus. This is the principle of spiritual multiplication, and this is the method Jesus left us for the spread of the gospel.

## NOT *IF* YOU'RE CALLED, ONLY *WHERE* AND *HOW*

Gospel multiplication isn't like a roller coaster.

Before entering that dreaded long line, everyone has to measure up.

My youngest son is finally tall enough that he clears most of the barriers. It was one of his worst moments when the rollercoaster technician would stand him up by the little board and inform him that he was a half inch shy of being able to join his sisters on the ride.

But the gospel strategy of multiplication isn't like a roller coaster.

Gospel multiplication involves more than just those you think are elite, varsity-class Christians. It involves more than the people you say are blessed "with the gift of evangelism"—those people who somehow manage to have a word of prayer with the cashier at Food Lion and she ends up in tears.

Gospel multiplication is for every son and daughter of God.

In the church I grew up in, "missionary" was a sacred and scary title, reserved for the spiritual elite, the Navy SEALs of the Christian world. We considered them heroes, sat in awe through their slideshows, and gladly donated our money to their ministries.

But in a real sense, *every* Christian is a missionary.

Now I'm not trying to detract from those who are called to work cross-culturally to take the gospel to unreached areas. That is an important and special assignment. And if we want to reserve the formal word *missionary* for that particular calling, I'm fine with that. But while not all Christians are called to move to Mumbai, all Christians *are* called to leverage their lives and talents for the kingdom wherever they live *now*. God's calling into his mission is not a separate call we receive years after our salvation. It is not a "Green Beret" distinction for super-Christians. It is inherent in the call to salvation.

The call Jesus gave to Peter and Andrew ("Follow me and I will make you fish for people") is for everyone, not just those who feel a special tingly feeling while they pray. Or those whose Cheerios talk to them.

Another way to put it is this: The question is not *if* we are called to leverage our lives for the Great Commission.

The real question is *where* and *how*.

This belief made the gospel spread like a prairie grass fire in the book of Acts. At various points Luke (the writer of Acts) goes out of his way to show us that the gospel traveled faster around the world in the mouths of regular Christians than the apostles and full-time Christian workers could get it there. He notes, for example, that the first time the gospel left Jerusalem, not a single apostle was involved:

- The first international mission trip was taken in Acts 8, by Philip, a layman. The Spirit carried him to a desert road where he met an Ethiopian government official, and Philip led him to Christ.

- The church at Antioch, which served as the hub of missionary activity for the second half of the book of Acts, was not planted by an apostle but simply "some brothers," whose names Luke did not even bother to record—presumably because no one would have known whom he was talking about.

- Apollos, a layman (at least at the time), first carried the gospel into Ephesus, and unnamed brothers first established the church at Rome. These Christians didn't travel to Rome on a formal mission trip but were carried there through the normal relocations that come with business and life. As they went, they made disciples there and planted a church.

As church historian Stephen Neill notes,

> Nothing is more notable than the anonymity of these early missionaries. . . . Luke does not turn aside to mention the name of a single one of those pioneers who laid the foundation. Few, if any, of the great Churches were really founded by apostles. Peter and Paul may have organized the Church in Rome. They certainly did not found it.[1]

From this point on—in the book of Acts and in the history of the church—"ordinary" people are going to be at the front of the gospel movement.

The more you consider the earliest church-planting movements, the more astounding it gets. Of the three great church-planting centers in the first century—Antioch, Rome, and Alexandria—*none* of them were founded by apostles.

The lack of apostolic involvement, in fact, is almost a little humorous.

Consider the apostle Paul, for instance, whose ambition for the entire second half of Acts is getting the gospel to Rome. He's beaten, imprisoned, shipwrecked—*several times each*—and even bitten by poisonous snakes!

When Paul finally drags his tired, beaten-up body into Rome, according to Acts 28, who greets him?

Brothers.

Paul writes, "There we found brothers and were invited to stay with them for seven days. And so we came to Rome" (Acts 28:14 ESV).

I can just imagine Paul, after the grueling, months-long journey at sea, stepping off the ship on the coast of modern-day Italy. Suddenly he looks up to see a group of people on the dock holding up poster boards with his name on them and balloons.

"Paul! Hey, Paul! We heard you were coming! So glad you could make it. Do you want to join us this week for house church? Can you preach for us? Maybe even write us Romans a book?"

I can't imagine anyone who would have been happier to lose the race to Rome than Paul.

Gospel multiplication wins every single time.

It's simply a better strategy than putting all our eggs in the "one hyper-anointed apostolic figure everyone should come and listen to" basket.

## THREE CONVICTIONS THAT WILL CHANGE THE WORLD

Seeing the gospel movement multiply is not that complicated. The reality is, for those in church leadership, it's not going to be about us. Ordinary people have always been the tip of the gospel spear, and if we're serious about the gospel making inroads into the lostness around us, they must continue to be.

The story of Stephen occurs at a critical moment in the book of Acts. The gospel movement is stymied in Jerusalem, even though Jesus had clearly told the apostles he wanted his gospel carried to Judea, Samaria, and the ends of the earth.

Now it had been an exciting ride, to be sure. I mean, with all the miracles and baptisms and people getting struck dead in the offering and such, what doesn't sound exciting about that? But the bottom line is that the church still hadn't left Jerusalem.

All of that changed with the story of Stephen.

Stephen was not an apostle, and I believe Luke (the author of Acts) gives us Stephen's story, in part, as an example of what ordinary men and women in the church are supposed to look like, and, more importantly, what will happen in the world when they do.

Stephen's story reveals three convictions that shape his life, convictions that should be held deep in the soul of every believer.

### Conviction 1: God Wants to Use Me

We are first introduced to Stephen when he gets selected to help deliver food to widows so the apostles could devote themselves to prayer and the Word. The important thing to note there is that his job was not glamorous. He wasn't chosen to teach or appointed to lead any committees. He didn't write books or go on a speaking tour. He was not considered to be one of the theological leaders in the early church.

He was just a table waiter.

Basically he was the Meals On Wheels of the early church.

Yet Luke tells us that Stephen served so zealously and faithfully and his witness was so full of the Spirit that it got the attention of many in the community—including many of the Jewish priests. Winning over the Jewish priests (good) eventually provoked a riot (bad) that led to the explosion of the church outside the borders of Jerusalem (good).

Turns out Stephen was more important than we assumed.

And then Luke tucks in what Bible scholars say is the critical turning point in the Acts narrative. Unfortunately, most people read right over it:

> And there arose on that day [the day of Stephen's martyrdom] a great persecution against the church in Jerusalem, and they were all scattered throughout the regions of Judea and Samaria, *except the apostles*. . . . Now those who were scattered went about preaching the word. (Acts 8:1, 4 ESV, emphasis added)

Luke goes out of his way to show us that the first time the gospel leaves Jerusalem, going into Judea, Samaria, and the uttermost parts of the earth, apostles were not involved. The service and witness of a "layman" provoked the riot, and the emissaries that went out from Jerusalem preaching the gospel did not include a single apostle in their number.

This pattern persists throughout the rest of Acts, indeed the rest of Christian history! The gospel travels faster around the world in the mouths of ordinary people than it does from the journeys of apostles.

**The gospel travels faster around the world in the mouths of ordinary people than it does from the journeys of apostles.**

Ordinary people have been, and will continue to be, the tip of the gospel spear.

What would happen if the folks in our pews started to see their skills as tools God had given them for the spread of the gospel?

The book of Proverbs notes, "Do you see a man skillful in his work? He will stand before kings!" (Prov. 22:29 ESV). Many of our people have excellence in a skill that can open doors and put them before *kings*. That skill may be in architecture, education, law, medicine, or numerous other fields. God has put into their hands the key to the nations.

What if we made our *primary* consideration in where we pursue our careers *where* we can be used in the mission of God? We teach our people that following Jesus means "whatever you are good at, do it well for the glory of God, and do it somewhere strategic for the mission of God." Lots of factors go into where we choose to pursue our career—where the money is good, where our extended family lives, where we want to live—and these are all valid.

*But why wouldn't the kingdom of God be the largest factor?*

John Piper points out that Lot's primary consideration in where to pursue his career was where he could make the most money. The plains of Sodom.

It did not turn out well for Lot.

Mission, not money, is the primary motivator for the follower of Jesus, regardless of his or her career path.

We tell students at our church, "You have to get a job somewhere. Why not get one in a place where you can be part of a strategic work of God?"

Consider this: If you overlay a map of world poverty with a map of world evangelization, you will find that the areas most in need of business development are also the most unevangelized. Many of the most unreached places in the world—most hostile to Christian missionaries—have arms wide open to any kind of businessperson.

Missiologists frequently refer to the "10/40 window" (the area of the world located between the 10 and 40 degree latitude lines) in which the most unreached people groups live. For business leaders, the 10/40 window isn't a window at all. It's a wide open door.

Now, God may not call you to leave the United States. But if you're a believer, he is calling you *somewhere*—to follow him where he goes, as he seeks to make his name known. Whether you're an investment banker or a full-time pastor, a stay-at-home mom or an overseas missionary, God has a mission for you.

From Raleigh-Durham to Bahrain, the responsibility to think this way belongs to every believer.

I mentioned in the last chapter how we're up against a huge lack of missionaries and church planters. I read recently that there are about forty thousand evangelical missionaries in the world right now. Praise God for them, but that's a pretty tiny number when you stack it up against the *billions* of people who don't know Jesus.

But here's another statistic.

There are also two million Americans in secular employment outside of the United States. An enormous majority of these Americans—at least half—are Christians.

Are American Christians the only ones that can share the gospel cross-culturally? Absolutely not. Increasingly, we're seeing missionaries *from* the nations *to* the nations. But as most of my audience is American, let's think about what it might look like to mobilize ourselves to the mission God's given us.

One million American Christians work overseas. Now, if you're like me, your first thought when you hear that might be, "Yeah, but how serious are they about their faith?"

Let's just indulge yours and my cynicism for a second.

Out of the one million American Christians overseas, let's say that 80 percent of them are phonies. (That's pretty harsh, but hey, you started this.) That still means there are *two hundred thousand evangelical Christians* placed in different areas around the world. They are funded by American companies, so money isn't an issue. And they dwarf the number of missionaries we've sent out.

What would happen if we mobilized *them* to consider their position a God-given opportunity to share the gospel? We would increase our missionary force by 500 percent without spending another dime!

That's not even to mention that the fastest-growing part of the church now lives in the Global South and East Asia. What happens when *they* get mobilized?

I saw this happen with my own dad. Right after he retired from the textile company where he had worked for almost forty years, his company rehired him, for more money than he had made before, to oversee the development of some new factories in the 10/40 window. There he rubbed shoulders with Asian businessmen that our mission teams could never get close to on a mission trip doing English corners and passing out water bottles. He was instrumental in seeing a couple of them come to faith in Christ and part of helping establish a new church there.

Total cost to the church:

$0.

In fact, we made money on the deal because he kept tithing back to us the whole time he was over there.

So here's a radical proposal: if college students and retirees give us two years, *we'll change the world.*

Let me explain.

It's not every Sunday you find a bacon, egg, and cheese biscuit in the offering bucket. But that's what happened years ago when college students first began attending our church.

One weekend in 2003 about five college students visited. They pulled up in one car into the drop-off zone, parked it there, and then piled out. They liked the service, and because college students travel in herds, the next week they brought back 250 of their friends.

I think they all arrived in that same one car.

In a period of less than a month, our attendance doubled. And during that same time our weekly average giving increased by $13.48. College students add a lot of great things to the dynamic of a church. Enthusiasm. Optimism. Evangelistic zeal. But money is not one of them.

Back to the infamous biscuit.

After the first service an usher came up to me and in his hands was a bacon, egg, and cheese biscuit from Bojangles. One of the college students had placed it in the offering plate with a little note on it that read (charitably misquoting Acts 3:6), "Silver and gold have I none, but such as I have, give I unto you."

The leadership of our church realized something quickly. With such a huge influx of college students, we might not be the wealthiest church, but we would always have a large pool of potential missionaries.

At The Summit we've realized that college students are an integral part of our mobilization strategy.

Years ago we began to challenge our graduating seniors to let ministry be the most significant factor in determining where they would pursue their careers. We began asking our college students to spend their first two years after graduation pursuing their careers in a place where we are planting a church.

*"Give us two years and we'll change the world."*

Hundreds upon hundreds of students have answered that call. In fact, recent college graduates account for a third of the people we send on our domestic church plants. And now we've extended that same principle with the Southern Baptist Convention's "Go2 Initiative." This way every college graduate in every Southern Baptist church is challenged to give their first two years to the mission of God.

Are you a college student? A recent college graduate? If so, let me issue this same challenge to you.

You may not be a member of our church, so you may not move somewhere to be a part of a Summit church plant. But you do have to live and work somewhere, so as I ask our students at The Summit, I'll ask you: *Why not live and work in a place where you can be part of a strategic work of God?*

And for those of you entering retirement, why not look at this season where God has freed you from the burden of work to give two years investing in what he is doing around the world?

"But we've been saving our whole life so we can retire at the beach and I can play golf."

Seriously? That's how you want to spend the last twenty years—arguably the least encumbered years of your life—before you meet King Jesus? On vacation?

Jesus had some thoughts on this.

"We must do the works of him who sent me while it is day. Night is coming when no one can work." (John 9:4)

Sure, people at the beach need Jesus, too. God and lost people are everywhere. But don't you dare spend the rest of your life on vacation.

### Conviction 2: The Holy Spirit Fills Me

The thing that always strikes me about Stephen's story is his brazen confidence—confidence to stare down the religious elite and not blink even when they had picked up stones to throw at him.

That confidence came from Stephen's awareness of the fullness of the Spirit within him. "Filled with the Spirit" is the most common characteristic repeated about him in Acts 6–7.

Do you want to know what gives ordinary believers extraordinary confidence? It's not grit.

It's not even Bible knowledge.

It's not a lot of social media followers.

It's the *knowledge* of the power of the Spirit within them.

All Christians *have* the power of the Spirit, of course. It's our birthright in Jesus. But it is the knowledge—the intimate awareness—of that power that makes the difference.

Jesus made such extraordinary promises about the power and potential of the Spirit in believers' lives, even though we may be tempted to think he was exaggerating.

For instance, consider the promise Jesus gave to his disciples later in Matthew 11:11: "Among those born of women there has not risen anyone greater than John the Baptist; yet whoever is least in the kingdom of heaven is greater than he" (NIV). "Least in the kingdom" means you know the least about the Bible. It means you have the least talent. It means you're the least eloquent. It means you have the least number of spiritual gifts.

Statistically speaking, that's got to be somebody. Maybe somebody reading this book. I'm not trying to be mean, just mathematically, somebody has to be at the bottom.

Right now you are thinking, *Hey, maybe it's me.* And maybe you're starting to feel sorry for yourself.

Don't.

Based on what Jesus said in Matthew, even you, bottom-of-the-pile guy, have more potential for power in ministry than John the Baptist because you (a) know the truth about the resurrection (which John didn't fully know) and (b) you have the Holy Spirit *permanently* dwelling in you, neither of which John had. (John was under the Old Testament dispensation of the Spirit, which did not include the permanent indwelling New Testament believers enjoy.)

That means it's no longer about your abilities in ministry. It's about your availability to be used by the Holy Spirit. God, you see, can accomplish more through one willing vessel than all the talent in the universe.

Do we believe that?

Here is just one example from Acts. This story immediately follows the story we read earlier concerning Stephen.

Philip, another ordinary guy—not an apostle—feels moved by the Spirit to go up to a remote region. He obeys and finds himself on a dusty road alone, probably wondering why he is there. Suddenly a chariot arrives carrying someone we now refer to as the Ethiopian eunuch. The eunuch is reading from the book of Isaiah. But he is confused. Philip climbs up into the chariot and leads him to Christ. Eusebius, the third-century church historian, tells us that the eunuch goes back to sub-Saharan Africa, where he is from, and plants a church that is still in existence today.

Think about it.

Through one act of obedience by an ordinary guy, the Holy Spirit accomplished more for global evangelization than all the apostles have been able to accomplish in eight chapters of ministry.

On the world evangelization scoreboard, that's: Ordinary Guys: 2 / Apostles: 0.

God can accomplish more through one believer cooperating with the Holy Spirit than with the most dazzling array of talent assembled anywhere in the world.

So here's the question: Are *you* listening to the Holy Spirit? When is the last time you felt moved by him into ministry?

> **God can accomplish more through one believer cooperating with the Holy Spirit than with the most dazzling array of talent assembled anywhere in the world.**

Throughout the book of Acts, the Holy Spirit is mentioned fifty-nine times. And in thirty-six of those instances, he is *speaking*. Now, what is maddening about that is that it doesn't usually tell us *how* he speaks, which is frustrating for Type A folks like myself.

For instance, in Acts 13:2, just how did the Holy Spirit tell the church to separate Barnabas and Saul for the work of the ministry? Skywriting? A liver shiver? Maybe a tweet from @RealJesusinHeaven?

For what it is worth, as maddening as it can be, I believe that ambiguity is intentional. Ambiguity about how God speaks encourages the humility we should possess in thinking we have heard from God. More havoc has been wreaked in the church following the words "God just told me . . ." than any other phrase. Absolute certainty should be reserved for the Scriptures.

But that is different from saying that God doesn't speak or move inside of us anymore.

Now I know that the moment I start talking about listening to the voice of the Spirit, objections start to crop up.

*Things were different back then!*

I acknowledge that. What the apostles were doing was, in profound and important ways, unique. But you cannot convince me that the *only inspired record* we have of the church following the Holy Spirit is completely filled with examples that have no relevance for our lives today. The Holy Spirit still convicts, still guides, still *speaks.*

We, as a church, need to listen.

Honestly, this is why Pentecostals have tended to buck the statistics when it comes to declining missionary numbers. Baptists—my little tribe of Christians—think we have the monopoly on missions. But statistically, they are better.

Why is that? Well, one missiologist explained to me this way: Baptists think they can best move people by painting a staggering picture of lostness in our world—which is important, of course. But hearing overwhelming statistics can be paralyzing.

Who wants to attempt to empty the ocean with a thimble?

Pentecostals, on the other hand, tend to say, "God wants me to go to *this* city and work among *this* people group."

Not everything from heaven has my name on it, but something *does,* and I am responsible for that.

Evidently, being gift driven is more empowering than feeling guilt driven.

### Conviction 3: As Jesus Was to Me, So I Will Be to Others

The most compelling part of Stephen's story, to me, is what he said as he died. Through his words we get a window into Stephen's soul, showing us what he was thinking about at the moment of his death. As the rocks pelted the life out of his body . . .

> He called out, "Lord Jesus, receive my spirit."
> And falling to his knees he cried out with a loud voice, "Lord, do not hold this sin against them." (Acts 7:59–60 ESV)

Where have you heard *those* two things before?

Well, they sound almost identical to what Jesus said when he died:

"Father, forgive them, for they know not what they do." (Luke 23:34 ESV)

"Father, into your hands I commit my spirit!" (Luke 23:46 ESV)

In Stephen's dying moments he was thinking about what Jesus had said on the cross—the very things Jesus had prayed for Stephen, Stephen is now praying for others.

In Stephen's dying moments he is attempting to do for others what Jesus had done for him.

To follow Jesus means to sacrifice your life for others like Jesus sacrificed himself for you.

Let me ask you a question: Where would you be without Jesus? Stop and answer that question. Where would you be right now? Where would you be headed in eternity?

Now consider this: that is precisely where millions upon millions of people in this world are without *us*. Jesus sent his church into the world *as the Father* sent him.

Seriously.

It's like Martin Luther said, "It wouldn't matter if Jesus died a thousand times if nobody ever heard about it."

That's why the apostle Paul said he considered himself a debtor to people who had yet to hear the gospel.

How do you become a debtor to people completely detached from your life? Simple—by taking seriously the implications of the gospel. Paul knew he was no more worthy of salvation than the millions of people who had never even heard about Jesus. He knew that it wasn't fair for him to receive so great a grace and do nothing about it. With belief in the gospel comes an obligation to multiply that gospel as far and wide as possible.

In other words, "What Jesus did for me, so I will do for others."

Once you realize what Jesus did for you on the cross, nothing in your life can look the same.

Your money.

Your house.

Your parenting.

Your career.

And for our churches, our primary objective is to see this ownership of the Great Commission assumed by our members.

God never called those of us in the church to maintain an institution. He called us to complete a mission. For that reason our question must always be: How can we take the resources and opportunities God has given us and leverage them so that the most people are reached with the gospel? If we focus our efforts on preserving our institutions instead of advancing the mission, God has every reason to take his hand off of us and move his Spirit elsewhere.

Have you wrestled with the obligations you owe to the gospel?

Have you squarely faced the fact that 2.8 billion people in the world have little to no access to the gospel? And don't turn that into a statistic, either.

Josef Stalin once reputedly said that the death of one is a tragedy, but the death of a million is a statistic. That's just not the case—as the fact that it comes from Stalin should confirm.[2]

Every one of those 2.8 billion people is like you and me. They are made in the image of God like you. They know what it is to be afraid like you. They have hopes and dreams and aspirations like you.

But they don't have the gospel like you.

As Jesus was to me, so I will be to others. The treasure he gave to us in the gospel demands to be shared.

We owe it to others.

## PASTORS, WE MIGHT BE THE PROBLEM

If sending and multiplication are so central to the gospel, they have to be at the center of everything our churches do. Multiplication must be so central that we say no to other *good* things if they compete with this one *essential* thing.

Ironically, the people most primed to stand in the way of this are church leaders themselves. I've said this before, but typically we like to measure success by "seating capacity," when gospel multiplication pushes us to measure our success by "sending capacity."

Seating capacity is comfortable. It's safe. But sending capacity is risky and frightening. Seating capacity makes the churches' leaders look important. But sending capacity makes the mission important.

Shifting from *seating capacity to sending capacity* will entail a radical shift in how many of us think about the mission of the church. But I believe it will also unleash the Spirit in radically new ways. We can use stellar talent and techniques to add to our church rosters. Or we can trust the Spirit to empower and equip our people for multiplication.

Multiplication is costly.

It hurts.

But the trajectory of discipleship is toward giving away, not taking in. As Dietrich Bonhoeffer famously said, "When Christ bids a man to follow, he bids him come and die." Jesus did not say come and *expand* but come and *die*. And he showed us what that means by his own example.

He brought life to the world not by gathering and elevating but by opening his hands and giving it all away.

Why would it surprise us that God wants to use the same process in our ministries? It is not through our *success* that God saves the world but through our *sacrifice*.

He calls us first to an altar, not a platform (Rom. 12:1–2).

His way of bringing life to the world is not by giving us numerical growth that enriches our lives and exalts our name. Instead, he brings resurrection out of death. As Jesus said,

"Unless a grain of wheat falls to the ground and dies, it remains by itself. But if it dies, it produces much fruit" (John 12:24).

We live by losing.

We gain by giving away.

What *we* achieve by building our personal platform will never be as great as what *God* achieves through what we give away in faith.

## EARLY CHURCH EXPLOSION

By the year AD 300, those two fishers of men Jesus called to leave their nets had multiplied into *millions* of believers in the Roman Empire. And in AD 312, even the Roman emperor got baptized.

Jesus and his band of ragtag disciples multiplied into an unstoppable movement. Without funds. Without celebrities. Without several of their people in the Senate.

Historian Rodney Stark asks, "How was it done? How did a tiny and obscure messianic movement from the edge of the Roman Empire dislodge classical paganism and become the dominant faith of Western civilization?"[3]

Wait for it.

*Multiplication.*

The early church exploded not by maintenance. Not by addition. But by multiplication.

If we want to see a similarly explosive movement of Christianity in our day, we need to adopt the same methods.

We won't get there by simply *maintaining* our churches, trying to hang onto our members by catering to their whims and preferences.

We won't get there by *addition*. Impressive platforms for impressive preachers can be, on occasion, used by God, but they are not the evangelization plan that Jesus left us.

We can't fall into the trap of *ministry professionalism*. According to Paul, the "work of ministry" belongs to the ordinary "saints," not the pastors (Eph. 4:12). That means that those of us on church staffs *left ministry*, in one sense, when we became pastors. We're no longer the ones doing ministry; we're equipping the saints in our churches and releasing them to do the ministry. We're backstage.

---

**The only way we get where we want to go is by *multiplication*. Not by gathering members and hanging on but by empowering them and giving away.**

---

The only way we get where we want to go is by *multiplication*. Not by gathering members and hanging on but by empowering them and giving away. By equipping and releasing fishers of men into the world, carrying with them the one word that's powerful enough to soften hard hearts, to bring reconciliation and forgiveness, and to bring spiritually dead people back to life.

*The gospel.*

# CHAPTER 5

# GOSPEL
# HOPE

*"The future is as bright as the promises
of God. . . . Expect great things from God,
attempt great things for God."*
–William Carey

George Lucas didn't believe in *Star Wars*.

During the final stages of filming for *Star Wars: A New Hope*, Lucas didn't think the movie would amount to anything at the box office. He thought it would be a cosmic flop. The same way I feel before 90 percent of the messages I preach.

He wasn't alone. Movie studios predicted Star Wars would be–as the kids say these days–an "epic fail."

Moviegoers felt differently.

*A New Hope* opened on May 27, 1977.

It actually came in second place at the box office that weekend, just behind *Smokey and the Bandit*. Ask your kids if they've even heard of that one. The original Trans-Am from that movie is now in the Country Music Hall of Fame in Nashville, and

I was stoked when I stumbled across it . . . and my kids were utterly disinterested.

Sure, *Smokey and the Bandit* earned $2.7 million opening weekend, whereas *A New Hope* only garnered a measly $2.5 million. But *Smokey* showed on 386 total screens.

*A New Hope?*

Only forty-three.

Those who watched it came back a second and third time and couldn't wait to bring back their friends.

By 2016, the Star Wars empire had earned close to $30 billion. In *The World According to Star Wars,* Cass Sunstein explains that Star Wars' total earnings exceed the GDP (gross domestic product) of nearly one hundred of the world's nations.

As Yoda might say: Quite profitable, it was.

As a ten-year-old boy, I don't remember being gripped by many things that felt like they were as life-and-death, galaxy-shaping important as Princess Leia's holographic opening SOS message to Obi-Wan Kenobi was.

"Help me, Obi-Wan Kenobi—you're my only hope."

As a ten-year-old, I was ready to offer my life in service.

That phrase did something to me. Beautiful Leia was in trouble, and only a man named Obi-Wan, stuck on the backside of a desert planet with two suns, could help. Who could have imagined Leia's phrase was about to usher us into a franchise that would gross more money than half the countries on earth?

After her death in 2016, *Rolling Stone* shared Carrie Fisher's ten greatest *Star Wars* moments. Topping the list? This quote.

> It's just a tiny blue image projected from R2-D2 in Luke Skywalker's garage, repeating that mysterious phrase over and over. But this was more than just the message that set the plot of the original *Star Wars* trilogy in motion; this was a sort of magical incantation, one that promised desperation and heroism, saviors with strange names and stakes as big as that whole far-away galaxy. . . . She sold every

bit of George Lucas's jargon-heavy, sketched-out worldbuilding like she was delivering a Shakespeare soliloquy.[1]

The empire-oppressed galaxy's only hope for freedom was the power of the Jedi.

As C. S. Lewis explained, fantasy tales like Star Wars capture our hearts because they resonate with the true saga God created us to participate in. Our adventure may not include "the Force" or the *Millennium Falcon* or Chewbacca, but it does promise its own "desperation and heroism, saviors with strange names and stakes as big as that whole far-away galaxy." We fight a battle against principalities, powers, and rulers in high places, a battle which not even lightsabers can help and for which we need "the full armor of God" (Eph. 6:11). The power of Satan's evil empire is great, and he has his death-star gamma gun aimed right at us.

Who is our Obi-Wan Kenobi?

Who will come and help us?

Do we have a hope?

## LOOK AT THE STARS, YOUNG PADAWAN

My wife says I am an annoyingly optimistic person. She's not sure why. Maybe it has something to do with genetics. Maybe it was the positive environment in my home during my first few years. Maybe the alignment of the two suns on Tatooine on the night of my birth. Whatever it was, my temperament seems primed for the bright side.

I can already tell this chapter is going to be *awesome*.

Can't you?

At any rate, it was a big deal for me, thirteen months into my missionary service in Southeast Asia, that I had become utterly dejected. I was frustrated at how little progress I was making in bringing the gospel to this unreached people group. By little, I mean none.

Well, that's not exactly accurate.

I had seen two people come to Christ during my time overseas. But both were wavering, and it seemed like everything I had worked for was crumbling along with their faith.

It wasn't for lack of effort on my part, however. On most days I spent most every minute of sunlight traveling to friends' houses, sharing stories from Scripture, and initiating dozens of gospel conversations. I was praying with more desperation than I ever had in my entire life. My missionary roommate even lodged a complaint with our superior that I was trying to do too much and forcing awkward gospel moments into conversations where they didn't fit. If the task had been contingent on my frenetic pace, then that city should have been seeing an Acts-level revival.

And yet, day after day, I saw nothing. It seemed as if I were throwing my gospel seed on the asphalt of a highway. I even considered going home early, convinced that everything I was doing was a waste of time.

That's when an older missionary named Dr. Keith Eitel took me aside and pointed up toward the sky.

"There," Dr. Eitel said, "you'll find a reason to press on."

I had no clue what he was talking about, but I didn't want him to *know* I had no clue what he was talking about.

So I dutifully scanned the horizon from one side to the other. Slowly. I even squinted my eyes and nodded as if I had seen something significant. As the Jedi's strength flowed from the forest, maybe the missionary's strength flows from the stars. I wasn't going to botch my Yoda moment like Luke did his, so I acted like I understood.

But I was still clueless.

"J. D., these are the same stars Abraham looked at thousands of years ago," Dr. Eitel said. "This is the same sky. And do you remember God's promise to him? He told Abraham that his descendants would be more numerous than these stars."

Dr. Eitel paused a moment, then looked at me.

"What God told Abraham was impossible. Abraham knew that. God knew that. *You* know that. But look at these stars.

These stars stand for people Abraham would never know—people like you and me—that believed the gospel. When he looked up at these stars, he was looking into the future and seeing you, me, and millions of others.

"J. D., I know you've seen nothing happening here. The work is hard. It's actually harder than you know.

"It's *impossible.*

"But God's promise is as sure today as it was for Abraham. And if God can bring life and a fruitful nation out of Abraham's dead body, he can surely raise to life the hearts of the Muslims in this city. In this sky tonight, among these stars, are the names of many of the people you have been praying for and sharing with. You may never see them follow Jesus, just like Abraham never saw *you* follow Jesus. But you can be absolutely sure that God isn't done here."

God is faithful.

He will complete the work he began.

He's promised that.

His promise is my hope.

## WHAT GOD CAN DO WITH A MOMENT

I never saw that explosion of conversions in that unreached people group in Southeast Asia.

Someone will. And I'll get to be a part of that story.

When and how it comes, we can't exactly predict—the moving of the Spirit is, as Jesus said, mysterious like the wind—but when it comes, we'll see God do more in a few moments than we can accomplish in a few thousand lifetimes.

The writer of Psalm 126 directs us to hope for this kind of awakening. In this wonderful little psalm, he describes two different kinds of spiritual awakening:

> Restore our fortunes, O LORD, like streams in the Negeb! Those who sow with tears will reap with songs of joy! He who goes out weeping, bearing the seed for sowing, shall come home

with shouts of joy, bringing his sheaves with
him. (vv. 4–6 ESV)

In verses 5–6, the psalmist talks about sowing in tears. This
is the slow way of ministry. The normal way, if you will. Israel
had many desert regions, and the psalmist is imagining soil
so dry that seeds planted needed to be watered individually,
watered with tears. Imagine how many hours of exhausting
patience and excruciating labor that would take!

God often works through us this way in the world: We
patiently plant the seeds of God's Word in the hearts of our
friends, our family, our neighbors, our teachers, and we water
them with our tears, and fertilize them with our faith. Seeing
the harvest takes *years* of faithful labor.

Think of Noah for a minute.

The apostle Peter describes Noah as a "preacher of righteousness" (2 Pet. 2:5).

Can you imagine it? Noah was told to build the ark 120
years before the flood came. Sometimes we can read the
account of Noah in Genesis and think that after God called
Noah to build the ark, the sky started to get cloudy and the rain
came forty-eight hours later.

But that's not what happened.

A year went by.

Two.

Ten.

Fifty.

A hundred.

It was as if Noah started preaching about a flood when
Theodore Roosevelt was president and just kept on going—"It's
just around the corner!"—*until today.*

What kind of hope and confidence must God have given
Noah! I get impatient in the drive-through line when I'm told
to just pull ahead and wait for my fries. I thought this was *fast*
food?

How do you respond when God calls you to something and there's a waiting period in between the calling and seeing the calling come to pass?

Yet Noah stayed the course. And all that time he was preaching to his neighbors. But none of them repented. *Zero converts in over a century.* It's hard to think of him as a successful preacher in any way, but Scripture holds him up as a model of faithfulness. It would do our hearts good to reflect on Noah and his labor of faithfulness and trust.

Or think of William Carey, the father of modern missions. He was largely opposed even by the Christians in England, who told him that his missionary zeal was misplaced. Despite the opposition Carey left for India in 1793. He worked with all of his might, but it was a full seven years before he saw his first convert. How many times, during those years, did he experience doubt?

*Perhaps they were right.*

*Maybe I should not have come.*

Robert Moffat was a nineteenth-century Scottish missionary to South Africa. He spent three years (1818–1821) just *traveling* to his assigned mission post. He and his wife labored faithfully for ten years but with no tangible results.

But then God began to stir within the people.

In a period of three years, the number of converts in Moffat's city went from zero to 120. How different things would have been if they had decided to abandon the work in year nine! Oh, friend, how we must ask God to grant us supernatural faithfulness!

Adoniram Judson is another example. Judson was one of the first American missionaries. He spent six years in Burma (modern-day Myanmar) before he saw his first convert—a man named Maung Nau. Judson confessed that even at the moment of Maung Nau's profession of faith, he was a bit skeptical because of the years of fruitlessness. He wrote in his journal:

> I begin to think that the Grace of God has reached Maung Nau's heart. . . . It seems

almost too much to believe that God has begun to manifest his grace to the Burmans; but this day I could not resist the delightful conviction that this is really the case. Praise and glory be to His Name forevermore.

I am also reminded of the British politician William Wilberforce. After his conversion in 1785, he labored for forty-eight years to abolish slavery in the British Empire. For much of his life, it must have seemed like a lost cause. The last stages of the Slavery Abolition Act of 1833 were carried out without him due to his declining health in the final years of his life. The act was passed just three days before his death, and he heard about it on his deathbed.

Nearly fifty years of faithful labor, and he nearly missed seeing the fruit of his faithfulness.

We could add to these stories those of Hudson Taylor in China, Jonathan Edwards with the Mohican Indians, and many others. They labor for years before seeing the fruit of their seemingly fruitless labor. Others, like Noah—and almost Wilberforce—never live to see the impact their faith in Christ produces.

But all of them had to endure years of barrenness.

I'm sure they all wondered—as I did—*Am I disconnected from the Spirit? Am I in sin? Did I actually miss God's will for my life?*

Author and Bible teacher Beth Moore once explained that what is true in the ecological realm is true in the spiritual. Not only must the planting of spiritual seeds be done intentionally, but planting and harvesting don't happen simultaneously.

> **As we sow spiritual seeds, God acquaints us with the discipline of waiting.**

As we sow spiritual seeds, God acquaints us with the discipline of waiting.

Just as farmers understand the process of planting seasons and harvesting seasons, so too must those planting and sowing spiritual seed.

As Psalm 126 says, sometimes God brings the harvest through our patient planting of seeds one by one.

Stories of faith heroes who keep on even when it doesn't look like anything is happening function like the voice of Dr. Eitel to me, strengthening my resolve and reminding me that no matter how hopeless the situation is at the time, no sacrifice made for Christ and for the gospel is ever made in vain.

But God works another way too.

### *"Like Streams in the Negeb"*

Occasionally, into this arid Negeb desert poured torrential rains that covered the plains, and streams overflowed the land. When the waters receded, it left a saturated and supple soil over which greenery spread like a carpet.

I can see the BBC *Planet Earth* time-lapse footage now.

The psalmist imagines God doing this to the hearts of the wayward Israelites. This is what happened, for instance, when Jonah (reluctantly) preached in Nineveh. It was a terrible sermon of only eight words with no clear outline, no illustrations, and no funny introduction. And Jonah was ticked at the people he was preaching to; he didn't even want them to believe.

Worst. Sermon. Ever.

Yet God did more in a moment through a shoddy sermon than a thousand impressively gifted missionaries armed with the best resources could have done in ten lifetimes.

Most often God works in seasons. But sometimes he works in an instant.

This is what the psalmist yearns for in Psalm 126. This yearning didn't negate his responsibility to plant the seeds and patiently water them with tears, but it does give him a hope that he refuses to relinquish, a hope that God will again send his Spirit into the land like a flood.

We can never give up that hope for our day either.

*Help us, Lord Jesus. You're our only hope.*

D. Martyn Lloyd-Jones said:

> [We] can fight and sweat and pray and write
> and do all things, but . . . [we are] impotent,
> and cannot stem the tide. We persist in think-
> ing that we can set the situation right. We start
> a new society, we write a book, we organize a
> campaign, and we are convinced that we are
> going to hold back the tide. But we cannot.[2]

But then, Lloyd-Jones says, we remember the promise:
"When the enemy comes in like a flood, it is the Lord who will
raise, and does raise the banner."[3]

Lloyd-Jones quotes from Isaiah 59:15, where Isaiah was
using battle imagery from his day. Advancing forces raised a
flag to signal when the army should move forward. When in
retreat—if the enemy army flooded in and pushed your army
backward—you lowered that flag. But when you regained
momentum and began again to advance, you raised the flag
back up.

Isaiah looks forward to times when God would so empower
his people to succeed in their mission that they raise up their
own flag—no longer on the defensive but advancing quickly
against the enemy. Lloyd-Jones continues:

> And so we throw ourselves upon the mercy
> of God. It is not so much an organized prayer
> emphasis as it is an act of desperation. And
> then, and only then, does the power of the
> Holy Spirit come flooding upon us and into
> us. And he does in a moment what incremental
> organization can hardly accomplish in half a
> century.[4]

I love that last phrase. Love it, love it, *love* it. I feel my heart
flooding again with new hope even as I write it: "He does in a

moment what incremental organization can hardly accomplish in half a century."

Jonathan Edwards, who oversaw the largest religious awakening among Western peoples in modern history as he led the first Great Awakening, said that at the beginning a few sermons were preached, a few mission efforts were organized, and a few converts were made.

"But then," he said,

> God in so remarkable a manner took the work into his own hands, and did as much in a day or two that, under normal circumstances took the entire Christian community, using every means at their disposal, with the blessing of God, more than a year to accomplish.[5]

He's talking about the streams of the Negeb.

Tim Keller says a revival is merely "the intensification of the normal operations of the Holy Spirit (conviction of sin, regeneration and sanctification, assurance of salvation) through the ordinary means of grace (preaching the Word, prayer, etc.)."[6] He's not typically doing a "new" thing as much as he is pouring great power on the "normal" things faithful Christians are already doing.

Prayers become more intense.

Worship becomes more joyous.

Repentance becomes more sorrowful.

And the preached Word yields greater effect.

The Spirit of God multiplies the effectiveness of our "normal" work of seed planting, bringing a bountiful harvest. And he does more in a moment than we can accomplish in a lifetime.

## WOULD YOU SHUT UP ABOUT . . .

I once heard a pastor say that the primary obstacles to God's next move are those who had front-row seats to his last one. Rather than letting God's extraordinary acts in the past inspire us to believe him for new ones in our present, we idolize the leaders, the times, and the methodologies. Then we lament that it will never be that way again. We make the movement-killing mistake of thinking God's great outpourings of power are behind us.

Evidently, that's what the people in the prophet Amos's day had done, and God rebuked them by telling them he was tired of hearing them boast about his glories in the past:

> This is what the LORD says to Israel: ". . . Do not seek Bethel, do not go to Gilgal, do not journey to Beersheba. . . . Seek the LORD and live." (Amos 5:5–6 NIV)

Now that may sound to you like a random list of ancient Middle Eastern cities, but it wouldn't have sounded that way to Israelites in Amos's day.

Here's what that verse might sound like today.

God might say, "Do not seek me in the upper room in Jerusalem, the halls of Wittenberg or Geneva, or in Charles Spurgeon's Metropolitan Tabernacle."

You see, at *Bethel*, Jacob had his life-changing encounter with God (Gen. 35:15).

At *Gilgal*, the children of Israel emerged from their forty-year wandering in the wilderness, believed God, and took possession of the Promised Land. There God "rolled away the reproach," renewed the covenant with them, then parted the waters of the Jordan River and knocked down the walls of Jericho (Josh. 5:9 NIV).

At *Beersheba*, God first gave to Abraham possession of the Promised Land (Gen. 21:22–34).

Each of these places represented a time when God moved in mighty power, when heaven touched earth. The Israelites knew about them and talked fondly about them.

Evidently, Israel got into the habit of thinking God's great outpourings of power were mostly a thing of the past.

"Wouldn't it have been awesome to be there when father Jacob got his vision of heaven?"

"To march with Joshua's armies and see God tear down the walls of Jericho?"

God said to them, in effect, "Would you shut up about Bethel? I am sick of hearing about Gilgal! Seek me now—in *your* generation—and live. I want to move in your day. I am not just the God of the past; I am the God of the present and the future. My name is not *I was*. It is *I am*."

I wonder if in our day God might be saying something similar to us.

Stop glorying in the Great Awakening.

Stop romanticizing the early church.

Stop idolizing Martin Luther.

Stop lionizing Charles Spurgeon.

Monuments to God's past works are important, but they should serve primarily as catalysts for faith in his present willingness.

When they don't, our admiration of his glorious works in the past *wearies him*.

This is one of the great dangers of being in a church or a denomination with a rich history.

If you've been part of a movement where God did some amazing things, you probably hear a good amount about "the good old days." No one ever *says* that God's best work is already done. But they act like it.

Let me prove it.

Think about the moment you have seen God move most clearly and powerfully. What sorts of things were you doing? Probably . . .

*You felt desperate.*

*You felt out of control.*

*You prayed a lot.*

*You trusted God's strength over your own.*

Contrast that with the spirit of those of us—yes, I'm indicting myself here, too—who have already seen "ministry success"

(a phrase that really should be stricken from public record).
How are we feeling *now*?

Do we feel that same sense of desperation *now*?

Or do we feel secure from the stability our successes have
brought us?

I'm all for celebrating the movement of God in our churches
and even building the occasional monument. But not if it keeps
us from looking forward in faith, from crying out to God with
desperation, from anticipating that another great movement of
God *is just around the corner.*

Whether your church is growing or dying, composed of
twenty people or twenty thousand, God's greatest works are not
behind you but ahead of you.

*They have to be.*

Here's how I know: there are still more than four thousand
unreached people groups in the world, and Jesus told us that
before history ends, a thriving gospel witness will exist in each
one (Matt. 24:14; Rev. 5:9). God's going to move in somebody to
see a harvest of conversions among those four thousand groups.
History can't end until the commission is complete. That means
great days of power are ahead for the church.

So believe, hope, and ask!

Study the past movements of God's Spirit, celebrate them,
learn from them, *and then move on from them.* God's greatest
works are in the future.

You probably have neighbors,
friends, and family members who
have yet to hear or believe the
gospel, and you might be deeply
burdened for them. If so, that
burden proves God is not done
working on earth.

So believe, hope, and ask!

This is not a time to hunker
down and wait for the end. This
is not a time to sit around our

> **This is a day for
> radical, audacious
> faith.**
>
> **This is a day for
> bold, believing
> prayers bathed in
> gospel-fueled hope.**

living rooms talking about how great things were in a previous generation. God is bringing life right in front of you! He's moving in power here and now. He's going to move tomorrow and next year.

This is a day for radical, audacious faith.

This is a day for bold, believing prayers bathed in gospel-fueled hope.

Believe.

Hope.

*And ask!*

## THE PROMISE, NOT THE PREACHER, IS THE HOPE OF THE WORLD

We've all heard plenty of things recently about the state of the church in America to discourage us. A staggering number of high-profile leaders, often known for their doctrinal conservatism and/or their ministry ingenuity, have fallen in severe immorality. Many abused their power for sex, and some covered up these horrid assaults. Others stole from their ministries. Others allowed unchecked arrogance and an out-of-control temper to make them cruel to their subordinates.

If you had asked me a decade ago to name the top ten young ministry leaders in the United States, I would have given you a list that now has half the names crossed off.

That's probably why I've found myself returning to Jesus' audacious promises to his apostles in Matthew 16 for hope again and again.

After Peter confesses Jesus to be the Messiah, Jesus responds,

> "Blessed are you, Simon son of Jonah, because flesh and blood did not reveal this to you, but my Father in heaven. And I also say to you that you are Peter, and on this rock I will build my church, and the gates of Hades will not overpower it." (Matt. 16:17–18)

Jesus here injected into his disciples a hope-filled vision of the future but a hope based not on the quality of the leaders. Instead, the hope was grounded in the surety of his promises.

He said, "*I* will build my church." Not, "You will build my church," but *I* will do it.

His promise, not Peter's faithfulness, would be the foundation on which this movement would be built. In fact, Jesus had just called Peter "Satan" for trying to talk him out of going to the cross! (Matt. 16:23).

I mean, let's be real.

Calling someone "Satan" has to be at the top of Jesus' list of insults. Yet not even Peter's diabolical confusion could hinder what God wants to do.

God will accomplish his purposes.

It is the unbreakableness of his promise, not of Peter, that is the hope of the church.

Of course, that's no license for complacency. Because while we are sure God will accomplish his purposes, what is not guaranteed is that he'll use *us* to accomplish those purposes.

It's not like he needs us. Evangelicals would be wise to realize that if God chose to use another group of believers to accomplish his mission, we would not be the first people God had set aside. The Jews of Jesus' day assumed God would never set them aside. God needed them! Right? But Jesus warned them, "The kingdom of God will be taken away from you and given to a people producing its fruit" (Matt. 21:43).

He gives the same warning to us.

The grace of God is amazing, but woe to us if we ever take it for granted (Rom. 2:4).

The recent acceleration of Christian leaders falling from ministry is, I believe, God trying to wake us up. He will not allow sin to go unchecked in his church, and if we don't repent, he will take his hand off of us and our children. He will not abandon his purposes, but he will find someone else.

I want my kids and grandkids to grow up in a country where God is moving in his church. But that won't happen if we turn a blind eye to rampant sin.

Even those of us who aren't guilty of public moral scandals have to acknowledge that evangelicals have lost a lot of moral authority in recent years because of our apparent willingness to wink at sin when it serves our interests.

Sometimes we've been willing to cover up (or minimize) abuse to protect our reputation, even when doing so endangered other victims. Other examples can be found in our recent approaches toward politics. Who can't be pained to see the erroneous arguments many evangelicals have used to justify the moral failings of political candidates lacking integrity, simply because those candidates served our interests? After loudly proclaiming to our society that "character matters," it seems that we are willing to give a free pass to those who champion our cause.

We are scared to speak out against sin in our camp for fear it might give ground to the agenda of our enemies.

But our enemy is Satan, and covering up sin *always* advances his agenda. Our cause is the gospel, and exposing sin, decrying it, and lamenting it always advances *that* cause.

To be clear, I'm not arguing here that Christians can only vote for perfect candidates. In fact, it's not primarily the *voting* I'm talking about. My concern is how easily evangelicals have attempted to minimize things we clearly know from Scripture grieve the Spirit of God because we think being silent works in our favor.

It seems that we evangelicals have approached politics with a single goal—*tactical victory*. And in the process we've succumbed to the age-old temptation of a lust for power.

Our witness is more important than a political seat at the table.

Our weapons are not the weapons of the world.

The gospel should trump political opportunism every single time.

Honesty and humility invite the presence of God. Political posturing and the minimization of sin drive him away.

Again, this is not about voting for candidate A or candidate B. How we vote matters, and that's a great discussion I hope you care about. But this is about how willing we are to wink at sin in our midst.

The apostle Paul tells us, under no circumstances, to wink at sin.

> But sexual immorality and any impurity or greed should not even be heard of among you, as is proper for saints. (Eph. 5:3)

As John MacArthur said in a recent interview, "it may just be that we *wink at* the sins of our chosen political leaders because we tolerate them among ourselves."[7] The people who approve of public sin, MacArthur claims, are probably the people who *practice* that sin, too. Or, to quote Senator Ben Sasse, our politicians don't make our country immoral; they just take advantage of where it already is."[8]

We must come to terms with our desire to court the favors of an earthly savior and how that keeps us quiet about things that grieve the Holy Spirit.

This is not the way of Jesus.

If he is our only hope, we have to do things his way.

## GREATER HOPE

Thank God Jesus' promises weren't conditioned on our fitness. Thank God the hope of the church is not in the quality of its leaders. Because the grace of God is our hope, even when the preacher falls, the promise remains.

*We* are not God's "last best hope on earth."

We are not Obi-Wan Kenobi.

He is.

In one of my favorite stories from the Gospels, a Canaanite woman comes to Jesus asking for healing for her daughter, who is being tormented by a demon. Jesus' initial response is harsh: "It isn't right to take the children's bread and throw it to the dogs" (Matt. 15:26). But the woman is unflinching because she knows he isn't speaking to her gender or her race; he is speaking to her unworthiness. So she responds with desperate faith in his grace: "Yes, Lord . . . yet even the dogs eat the crumbs that fall from their masters' table" (Matt. 15:27).

In other words, the grace of God is so abundant that it flows off of the table such that even those with no more worthiness than a dog can eat until they are satisfied.

This Canaanite got her miracle.

Jesus admired her faith.

And she is our example.

We can never hope too much in the grace of God. We can never lean too fully into it. Better to be dogs feasting on the crumbs from God's table than "heroes" asking God to reward us for our greatness or sustain us because of our legacy.

Downward dog is the best posture for the servants of God.

## THE FUTURE IS STILL AS BRIGHT AS THE PROMISES OF GOD

Make sure this sinks in: the task Jesus gave Peter in Matthew 16 was not just daunting; it was impossible.

Just as impossible as changing Muslim hearts in Southeast Asia.

Just as impossible as producing a child from the loins of a hundred-year-old patriarch.

And that's good news.

Because the impossibility of the task can drive us in desperation to the promises of God, and no impossibility is too great for the power of those promises. Faith, Paul says, is trusting "the God who gives life to the dead and calls things into existence that do not yet exist" and being "fully convinced that what God had promised, he was also able to do" (Rom. 4:17, 21).

When I think about the future of the church, I often come back to the prophet Isaiah's words:

> Behold, the LORD's hand is not shortened, that it cannot save, or his ear dull, that it cannot hear; but your iniquities have made a separation between you and your God, and your sins have hidden his face from you so that he does not hear. (Isa. 59:1–2 ESV)

In other words, God's lack of compassion isn't why there's not more revival. God hasn't suddenly grown short on power or cold in love. The same Jesus that said, "Father, forgive them" from the cross still pleads for sinners before God's throne. The issue is not a deficiency in God's power. The same divine Spirit that brought Jesus back from the dead is at work in the world today.

The issue is us.

God still desires to extend his salvation to the ends of the earth.

He still has the power to do it.

And he still plans to use us.

The question is, Do we believe that, and are we prepared to open up ourselves to him and let him to move?

William Carey, in the midst of grueling trials he encountered bringing the gospel to India, wrote, "The future is as bright as the promises of God."

If you trust in Jesus' commitment to his church, your future, and the future of your church and your children, are as bright as the promises of God.

Because we know Carey's story—and, more importantly, because we know Jesus'—we can have hope in ours.

I can faithfully work at my job, even when I'm not seeing great results, because I know that one day God will fulfill all that he has promised.

Just like that little woodpecker.

He was tapping away at a telephone pole when lightning struck it and split it in two. Dazed, the woodpecker hovered for a moment in front of the split pole, and then suddenly flew away. He grabbed a few friends and brought them back, saying, "Yep, boys, there she is. Look at what I did."

I want that to be me.

I know, based on God's promises in Matthew 16:23, that he is not done with us. Like I said, there are still more than four thousand unreached people groups in our world. God tells us he will bless his people *for their sake*. He tells us that he desires to be merciful to us and bless us and cause his face to shine upon us—not for our sake but so that his way may be known in all the earth (Ps. 67).

**With the unchanging promises of God's Word as the foundation of our hope and the Holy Spirit as our guide, we can once again "expect great things from God and attempt great things for God."**

With the unchanging promises of God's Word as the foundation of our hope and the Holy Spirit as our guide, we can once again "expect great things from God and attempt great things for God."

The hope of Obi-Wan Kenobi (and later Luke Skywalker) created a culture of hope among the rebellion. With a few good leaders and a few small victories, they rallied behind the Rebel cause. They believed they had what it would take to bring down the *Deathstar*.

In Christ we have something better than Luke Skywalker and R2D2.

We have a Savior who won a decisive victory on the cross. And because you know he has won, you can be sure you will also.

This kind of hope does more than lift our spirits about the future.

This kind of hope changes our confidence in the present.

We find in God's promises the freedom to live with reckless abandon. Hope in God's promises sets us free to love, forgive, and serve others as Jesus has so graciously served us.

And because we are so confident in his goodness to us, that changes how we talk to one another—and about one another.

Gospel hope always produces a culture of extravagant and tender grace.

To that we now turn.

# CHAPTER 6

# GOSPEL
## GRACE

*"The greatest single cause of atheism in the world today is Christians: who acknowledge Jesus with their lips, walk out the door, and deny Him by their lifestyle. That is what an unbelieving world simply finds unbelievable."*
–Brennan Manning

Imagine eating dinner knowing the person across the table stands against everything you hold precious. She believes you are on the wrong path and that what you believe is destructive to you and everyone around you. That you are backwards, ignorant, a bigot, and an embarrassment. This they tell you regularly, both privately and publicly–having even gone so far as to write an op-ed about you in the local paper.

Now imagine inviting this person back into your home, again and again, in front of your children, so she can tell you that, on a regular basis.

Rosaria Butterfield says that a Christian couple's decision to do just this is what brought her to faith.

Butterfield, at the time a lesbian, living with her partner whom she deeply loved, a committed advocate for LGBT rights, and coauthor of the first domestic partnership policy at Syracuse University, explains that her goal was to gather first-hand research on the Religious Right, whom she believed to be not just anti-intellectual but anti-American. She didn't understand why Christians wouldn't just stop getting in the way of people living their lives in freedom.

She had solid intellectual backing for her convictions and was prepared to refute the ignorance behind the convictions of Pastor Ken and his wife Floy.

But she wasn't prepared to be treated with such compassion.

Butterfield explains that she was overwhelmed with the kindness they showed her and the genuineness with which this pastor, his wife, and their children loved her.

So she kept going back.

She couldn't help herself. Again and again. Month after month.

*For two years.*

Through the relationship with this couple, Butterfield experienced the love of Christ in the gospel. Through radical hospitality—as she describes it—and kindness, she saw the beauty of God.

The sad part for Christians today is that kindness and grace aren't always the words people use when they first think about us.

Abdullah is the Muslim chaplain at one of our local universities in the Raleigh-Durham area. Among the many things I like about Abdullah is his candor. Sometimes when I say something with which he disagrees, he just smiles and shakes his head and mutters, "Oh, no, no, no."

A few years ago Abdullah and I were invited to a religious debate at the University of North Carolina at Chapel Hill. Usually my role on these panels is to be the token "evangelical Christian," which for those in academia is roughly equivalent to being a real-life Neanderthal.

But sure enough seven hundred students showed up to see if Abdullah the imam and a local rabbi would dominate the neighborhood's chosen ~~knuckle-dragging, mouth-breather~~ evangelical.

The debate went well. If anything, I think people were hoping for more fireworks. It's not that Abdullah and I just smiled and agreed with each other. Quite the contrary. We were both abundantly clear that we thought the other was in error. We tried to show that. But we *liked* each other and treated each other with respect.

That debate spawned a several-year friendship that has included multiple meals, conversations, and family get-togethers. They've even come to our church's Christmas Eve service with us.

Shortly after our first debate, another university caught wind of how well ours had gone and wanted to host their own. This time Abdullah was invited but not me because the debate was hosted by a local, liberal private Christian university and they didn't want an *evangelical* representing Christianity. So they used one of their religion professors.

Abdullah called after it was over and wanted to process the debate with me. When I asked him how it went, he said, "Not good." "I think I am more Christian than that professor is."

I wasn't sure how to respond. I'm used to hearing Christians excommunicate each other. Hearing a Muslim excommunicate a Christian was new for me.

"What do you mean?" I asked.

"Well, every time the Bible came up, he seemed embarrassed. He spent more time explaining why it doesn't mean what it plainly says."

Then he said this:

"You know, pastor, it seems to me that your Christian world faces a dilemma. On the one hand are people who believe the Bible. And, on the news at least, this group seems to have an uncharitable spirit toward Muslims. On the other hand, we see Christians like this professor who don't believe the Bible, yet they have a charitable spirit toward us.

"Your Christian world feels like these are the two alternatives:

"Believe the Bible and be mean.

"Deny the Bible and be loving.

"And because most won't outright deny the Bible the way this professor did, they are forced to assume that believing the Bible must be accompanied by an intolerant, hateful spirit."

Gulp.

"What they need," Abdullah continued, "is what I see in you. You believe everything the Bible says. You believe that when I die I will not go to heaven. Even still, you have a charitable spirit toward me and my family and genuinely want to be my friend."

Abdullah is absolutely right, of course. But his idea isn't a very politically correct one.

The prevailing idea today is that the only path to peaceful dialogue is through compromise. Through holding your beliefs *less* strongly. The more we act like we all believe the same things, the more we'll get along. But as Abdullah knew, that's not dialogue. That's delusion.

> **Is it possible to believe in truth passionately and to accept others with grace?**

Is it possible to believe in truth passionately and to accept others with grace?

## GRACE *AND* TRUTH

Jesus was known as someone "full of grace and truth" (John 1:14). He possessed both in fullness, and it made him simultaneously intolerable and irresistible. He spoke with such clarity that his enemies could not rest until they had killed him. Yet he exuded such grace that many of those who disagreed with him still couldn't resist being around him.

What people experienced with Jesus is what Rosaria Butterfield experienced through her friendship with Pastor Ken and his wife, Floy.

Kindness that's irresistible.

Grace that's overwhelming.

Truth that's constant.

Failing in either grace or truth puts us out of step with Jesus.

Truth without grace is fundamentalism. Grace without truth is sentimentality.

To dispel the tension here, we must turn to perhaps Jesus' most misunderstood teaching.

## TO JUDGE OR NOT TO JUDGE?

I haven't done a systematic survey, but I'm pretty sure the most popular verse in the Bible today is Matthew 7:1, or at least the part of it most people know: "Judge not" (ESV).

I once typed in, "The Bible says not to . . ." on a Google search. Google auto-completed the five most popular items.

The Bible says not to . . . worry.

The Bible says not to . . . get tattoos.

The Bible says not to . . . eat. (This search made me wonder what Bible Google uses—certainly not a Southern Baptist one. I think the Bibles we sell at the SBC come with a coupon for 10 percent off at Golden Corral.)

Kidding.

But more popular than all those was, "The Bible says not to . . . judge."

I've even heard Bill Maher, not known for his scriptural savvy, quote it *at* Christians. There's something about that snappy little two-word command that seems to fit in with our societal mood. Specifically, it seems to capture two of our society's most basic assumptions: (1) religion is private, and (2) morality is relative.

People love "judge not" because it sounds like a handy way of saying, "You can't tell me I'm wrong." It's the non-Christian's best weapon to keep Christians off their back.

Can't argue with the Bible, right?

The problem is, Jesus–the one who, you know, uttered the words–didn't share our assumptions about the importance of keeping your opinions about morality to yourself. He was constantly making public judgments, many of them rather striking. He called some people's works evil (John 7:7). In Matthew he told a group of sincere people, "You are wrong, because you know neither the Scriptures nor the power of God." So he couldn't have meant "keep your ideas about religion and morality to yourself."

No, when Jesus denounced judging, he wasn't telling us to stop assessing opinions or behavior. Instead, he was telling us to avoid a graceless, critical posture that writes other people off, that tells them the truth and then pushes them away.

The kind of behavior Rosaria Butterfield expected.

Even though Jesus told people that they were wrong and their works were evil, John 3:17 says Jesus was not in the world to *condemn* the world but to *save* it.

Speaking a hard truth isn't the same as speaking condemnation.

Judging is not telling someone hard truth. Whether or not you judge is determined by what you do *after* you tell them truth.

---

**The antidote to judging is a culture saturated with gospel grace.**

---

Judging goes beyond speaking a hard truth–"This is wrong"–to saying, "I don't want you around anymore."

The antidote to judging is a culture saturated with gospel grace. A culture that feels like Jesus.

I believe there are seven signs that reveal that we live in a culture of judgment rather than gospel grace.

### 1. We're more enraged at someone else's sin than our own.

If you've been transformed by the gospel, your primary dismay is not with others' sins but your own. Dietrich Bonhoeffer said one of the first signs of Christian maturity was a frustration with the hypocrisy of the church and a desire to separate from it. But the *next* sign of growth was recognizing that the same hypocrisy in the church is present *in oneself.* We must confront others in their sin but always while being painfully aware of our own. The moment we find more offense in the sin of others than in the sin of our own hearts, the more we have left the realm of grace.

There will always be a vital role in the Christian life for confrontation. Jesus himself said, "If your brother sins, rebuke him, and if he repents, forgive him" (Luke 17:3). But, as Paul says, when we do so, we do so with the knowledge that we are made out of the same stuff they are and that if God marked our iniquities, none of us would have a leg to stand on (Gal. 6:2).

When the psalmist, for instance, asks for protection from sin, he asks to be held back from giving in to sins he wants to commit and committing sins he doesn't even know he's committing (Ps. 19:12). No matter how righteous you think you are, there is always sin you don't see. "Blind spots" and "areas of weakness" are not the same thing. Blind spots, by definition, are sinful places in your heart you don't even know about. If you did, you wouldn't be blind to them. Christian counselor Paul Tripp says that while we are blind to our own sin, others have 20/20 vision. We'd be wise to do more listening to others regarding our own sin than we do bemoaning theirs.

## 2. We refuse to forgive. Or when we forgive, we refuse to forget.

To refuse to forgive someone is to be intentionally ignorant of the enormity of what God has forgiven you. And to "forgive but not forget" is, as I've heard it said, "a distinction without a difference." It's just another way of saying, "I'm going to say I forgive you to make myself feel better but show that I really haven't by reminding you all the time of how much you still owe me because of what you did." That's not forgiveness at all. Forgiveness means absorbing the debt and offering only love and goodness in return with no strings attached.

## 3. We cut off those who disagree with us.

This is the *essence* of judging. When someone doesn't fit your "standard" of behavior or conviction, you refuse to reward them with your love or presence. Because you disagree with them, you take the further step of cutting them off. You say, in essence, "We can't really be friends if we disagree on this issue."

Think about it: the ultimate statement of judgment is, "Depart from me, you worker of iniquity."

Christians never say that to anyone because, well, they are not given the role of judge.

Jesus never even said that to anyone while on earth. He predicted that one day (in heaven) he would say that, but on earth, even after Judas betrayed him with a kiss, he called him "friend" (Matt. 7:23; 26:50).

We do what Jesus did. We speak truth and then offer kindness and love, constantly drawing them as close as they will let us. Even if it costs us our lives.

Jesus is saying that we have to love the person we disagree with more than we love their agreement on a particular issue. That doesn't mean we ever compromise or water down our position. It means we stay committed to, and in relationship with, those who passionately disagree with us.

## 4. We gossip.

Gossip is judging because it condemns, in a way, the person we are talking about. It doesn't redemptively invite them to better behavior (that's graceful confrontation); it dismissively writes them off as flawed and worthy of scorn. And what makes gossip so dangerous is that we are judging someone without even giving them the benefit of knowing we are doing it! We're not even offering them a chance to change. It's as if we don't even think they can change or that they're not worth the relational discomfort of confronting them so that they might. In some ways gossip is the ultimate form of judgment because it writes people off without even telling them. Even if you mask your gossip as a "prayer request" or soften it with that classically Southern "bless her/his heart." Everyone still knows what you're doing.

## 5. We refuse to correct someone's position.

Ironically, *not* telling people they are wrong is a way of judging them. As a Christian, when you refuse to correct someone, it's for one of two reasons: (1) you don't believe that the Bible is true, or (2) you don't think the other person can actually change. Neither one is honoring to God. As with gossiping, by assuming the other person *won't* change or *won't* listen, you're judging and condemning them from the start. You're consigning them to their sin without ever giving them the chance to receive grace. Remember, God has the power to do whatever he wants. The gospel-shaped heart never gives up that hope.

## 6. We refuse to receive criticism.

Ask yourself, "*Why* do I hate criticism so much?" Isn't it because you hate to admit you have faults? You see yourself more as "righteous one qualified to dispense judgment" than "sinner in need of grace." You think it more appropriate for you to play judge than to be judged.

But if you understand the gospel, your faults shouldn't surprise you. When others point out your depravity, you should be able to say, "Well, of course. In fact, I'm way more sinful than you've probably even noticed! But I'm not afraid of that because nothing can ever be revealed about me that the blood of Jesus has not already covered!" And that recognition will change how you point out the sins in others.

### 7. We write someone off as hopeless.

Writing off someone as hopeless means you think they are past saving. You declare judgment on them. Paul said the gospel was the power of God to salvation for *everyone* who believes. It's not our place to amend that.

If you're not dead, God's not done.

If they're not dead, there is still hope.

## GRACE SPILLING OUT INTO THE STREETS

A culture shaped by gospel grace does more than just *speak* to people with grace, however; it showers them with the generosity of Jesus.

As we've noted throughout this book, Christians are becoming less and less popular in our society.

Sorry if that has been a news flash to you. But studies show that people feel more comfortable talking to an IRS agent than an evangelical Christian.

Ouch.

Because of this, many Christians are ready to go to war. "It's time to show everybody we are the truly righteous ones."

Desperate times call for desperate measures, right? Who has time to be civil and kind when you're under attack?

But we don't look to our culture for our response.

We look to Jesus.

By looking to Scripture, we find the unchanging example of Christ, who "when . . . reviled, did not revile in return" (1 Pet. 2:23 NKJV).

Jesus did not conquer sin by fighting sinners. He conquered sin by dying because of it and rising from the dead to defeat it. On the other side of his death was the power of resurrection.

And he offers the same pattern to us.

Extending gospel grace means sometimes you'll often feel scorned and defeated in public. Misunderstood. Abandoned.

So did Jesus.

But remember that the way of the cross leads to resurrection power.

This pattern is more important now than ever. Our world is sick and in need of the healing balm of the gospel. We must aim for the same paradox Jesus embodied in his ministry.

Grace *and* truth.

Only that crucial gospel formula sets people free. We must not only speak the truth of Christ; we must do so with the spirit of Christ. Otherwise we lie about him—no matter what we are saying.

The gospel truth in our churches has to be matched by gospel generosity in the streets. If we can recover this paradox of grace and truth, we might just be surprised at the walls our society has built that come crumbling down.

Several years ago our church began to recognize that we had gotten this balance wrong. We were focused on proclaiming the gospel truth from our pulpit, but no gospel generosity was flowing out our doors. With the leading of the Spirit, we resolved to become a church that would bless our city. With our mouths. And with our hands.

In addition to planting other churches in the city, that meant discovering where our city was hurting and applying Christ's healing in those places.

So we began to ask the question: "Where can we bring great joy to our city as a demonstration of the gospel?"

I scheduled an appointment with the mayor and asked him to list out the five most underserved parts of our city so we could get involved there.

"Schools." That was his first answer.

And just like that, our local outreach ministry–ServeRDU–was born.

The beginnings were modest. Through one teacher we found out about a family in need of temporary housing. One of our church members, who was about to get married, asked his guests to redirect any wedding presents to this family to stock their house. We were allowed in to paint classrooms, scrub floors, and bring teachers breakfast. Then the principal invited us to come pray for the students during their end-of-grade exams, which led to a pretty extensive tutoring partnership between our members and at-risk kids there. After several years of our involvement, the school received a "most improved" award because their end-of-year grades were among the highest in the county.

This was what it meant to serve our city with grace.

By God's mercy and his power, ServeRDU continued to expand.

Years after that first visit, I was invited to speak at our city's annual Martin Luther King Jr. rally. Durham is 40 percent African American, so this event is a big deal. I agreed, but not being the typical candidate to keynote an MLK rally, I was a nervous wreck.

The county manager, sensing my anxiety, said something I will never forget.

"J. D., do you know why you were asked to speak today?"

"No sir," I said.

"It's because of how your church has blessed our city."

Another city official shared with me later that afternoon, "It seems that everywhere in our city we find a need, we also find people from The Summit Church meeting that need. And we couldn't think of anyone to better embody the spirit of brotherly love we want to honor on this day than you all at The Summit."

God has continued to renew our call to our city.

He has raised up new leaders in our midst to carry out new and innovative ministries. Our church–and *every* church—exists to serve the city, to bring joy to it, to spill God's grace extravagantly into the streets. And it is no surprise that this grace has opened doors to segments of our society that we would never have otherwise been able to reach.

As in, say, with our local prisons.

We've seen a steady stream of prisoners begin to attend our church every weekend through a program that allows inmates nearing the end of their sentences to get out for a few hours each weekend with families from our church who "sponsor" them. Many have accepted Christ. In fact, my favorite "giving" story of all time comes from a prisoner who sent $5 to us with this note:

"I know this isn't much, but it's 10 percent of what I have. I can't get to the membership class yet (for obvious reasons), but I already feel like a member of your church. I have been saved for the last eighteen months now, and I can see God changing my life. Your preaching is like Tupac's rapping—the raw, uncut truth, only in the pulpit."

That's not quite on the level of, "You preach like Billy Graham," but I'll admit, I was flattered.

Christians should be known for their excessive love toward their neighbors and the nations. There was a time when the grace of Christians was overwhelmingly evident to the surrounding community, and in those days the church's testimony was compelling. In the fourth century the Roman emperor Julian actually complained about kindness of the Christians in his day:

> How can we stop the growth of these wretched Galileans? They take care not only of their own poor, but ours as well!

What if *that* was the complaint our culture had against us? Wouldn't it be nice for the world to hate us for loving them too well? The county manager storms into the mayor's office and says, "*Daggum* it! We have to cancel another government program because those Christians have already met the need"?

If that sounds laughable to you, perhaps that's a sign of just how far we've fallen from the gospel.

Pastor Ray Ortlund, in his book *The Gospel*, notes that a culture of grace should naturally accompany gospel doctrine, and when it doesn't, something is deeply wrong, even if the words we use in our creed are exactly right.

> A church with the truth of the gospel in its theology can produce the opposite of the gospel in its practice. The risen Lord said to one of his churches, "You say, I am rich, I have prospered, and I need nothing, not realizing that you are wretched, pitiable, poor, blind and naked" (Rev. 3:17). The problem was not what they believed doctrinally but what they had become personally, and they didn't even realize it. Yet it was obvious to the Lord: "I know your work" (Rev. 3:15). Therefore, they needed to go to Christ with a new humility, openness, and honesty.[1]

Ortlund continues with this poignant statement: "Without the doctrine, the culture will be weak. Without the culture, the doctrine will seem pointless."[2] In other words, we can preach "Jesus in my place" all we want, but if it doesn't make our members say, "Let me bring the love of Jesus to *your* place," it won't be convincing to a world looking for a better story to believe in, a better community to belong to.

**Gospel doctrine that is not accompanied by gospel grace is deadly both to the culture and the church that is dispensing it.**

Gospel doctrine that is not accompanied by gospel grace is deadly both to the culture and the church that is dispensing it.

## GRACE SATURATING THE PEWS FIRST

Before gospel love can spill out into the streets, however, it must first saturate the pews. And, sadly, this might be the place we see it least.

The late Francis Schaeffer used to say that love on display was Christ's "final apologetic" to a skeptical world. Usually that is interpreted to mean we validate Christ's message by our excessive generosity toward outsiders. But specifically, Schaeffer was referring to the love that exists *between* believers. Jesus said this, too (John 13:35). He told us that the world would know we are his by the way we love *one another*.

Not first by the way we love *the world*.

By the way we love *one another*.

Some of those most zealous to impact the world with the love of the gospel overlook this crucial, family-first dimension of gospel grace. I once was part of a Bible study on Galatians where participants took turns teaching. The brother assigned to teach Galatians 6 got to verse 10, which says, "Let us work for the good of all, especially for those who belong to the household of faith," and then he said, "You know, I don't really agree with this. We should focus our good works on those on the outside, not people who are already Christians."

I admired his evangelistic zeal, but he was making a mistake many Christians make—overlooking the fact that Christlike love will be first expressed and lived out *in the church*. Well, that and thinking he is allowed to correct the Bible.

If love is not first lived out in the Christian family, how can it ever extend to the rest of the world? Grace can only *spill* out into the streets if it is first overflowing in the hearts of God's people, the church.

The church was created to be such a miracle of love that people from the outside could see the image of Christ simply in how we relate *to one another*. Mark Dever, a pastor in Washington, DC, calls this "making visible" the invisible Christ.[3]

I love that image.

It reminds me of my childhood fascination with super-heroes—a fascination that has only slightly ebbed in my adult years.

As a boy, I used to dress up like superheroes all the time. I was Batman, Superman, Spiderman . . . but never the Invisible Man. The closest I could come was going into my sister's room when she was away, messing her stuff up, and telling her the Invisible Man had done it. (She was less than credulous.)

But on the television show, when someone wanted to make the Invisible Man visible, they would pour paint on him. This allowed you to see his shape and track his movements.

That's what the church does for Jesus.

We are the paint poured over the life of the church that makes the invisible Christ visible. In its fellowship, its holiness of life, its cultural diversity, its selfless acts of love, and its forgiveness and boldness, the church reveals the contours of the eternal, heavenly, beautiful Christ that dwells within us.

To say it plainly: those who believe the gospel should look like the gospel. And that starts with how we relate to our brothers and sisters.

Unfortunately, I'm not sure the way we see Christians treat one another, especially in public and on social media, would generally be described as "full of grace and truth."

This topic may require a book of its own, but before I close this chapter, let me suggest five brief ways I believe gospel grace and generosity should shape our interactions with other believers, particularly in the midst of disagreement.

### 1. Give the benefit of the doubt.

Around our church offices we say this *all the time*. It's one of those statements we want our staff to be able to reproduce without even thinking about it. I tell our staff that if I were to break into one of their houses at 3:00 a.m. and rouse them from a deep REM, the first words out of his mouth should be, "Give the benefit of the doubt!" (The next words would probably not be fit for print in a Christian book.)

As we interact with others, there are literally thousands of opportunities to either *give* or *withhold* the benefit of the doubt. If we're letting the gospel shape our interactions, we should choose to give more often than we withhold.

I often tell our pastoral team something I first heard Jeff Bezos of Amazon explain: When conflict arises, assume two things about your coworkers: (1) they are smart, and (2) they have good intentions. If we're able to return to these two convictions often, 90 percent of conflict will disappear before it even gets started. But of course, these convictions aren't natural. In my experience the moment conflict begins, I inherently assume the opposite (that people are either dumb or evil). A new idea pops up that we think is a poor one. A new HR policy means more work. A great idea (of ours, naturally) doesn't get off the ground. In every one of these instances, we are tempted to assume that someone *out there* is a fool or a villain. Maybe both.

But the gospel counsels us to start by assuming the opposite: Love means "bearing all things, believing all things." That means starting with the assumption of the benefit of the doubt.

What does it say to the world when we are constantly bickering and name-calling among ourselves? Let's demonstrate a more excellent way.

### 2. Assume the best about others.

This idea goes hand in hand with the previous one, but it's so important, I thought I'd come at it from two angles. After all, a key to learning is repetition and redundancy and saying the same things over and over.

Assuming the best means accepting the best possible narrative about someone and their motives as we can. A Bible teacher I know says "assuming the best" means "filling in the gaps with trust." Here's how he described it:

We all know what it's like to face a gap between expectation and reality. Your son was supposed to arrive home at 10:00 p.m. (expectation), but he didn't walk in the door until 10:20 p.m.

(reality). An important project in your office goes live (reality) without anyone consulting you (expectation).

When we sense a gap, we have a choice.

Our natural tendency is to fill the gap with suspicion:

He was late because he doesn't respect me.

She didn't consult me because she thinks she has nothing to learn.

He said such-and-such because he's a bigot.

But cultivating a culture of trust means choosing to fill those motive-gaps with trust.

Lest you think this too difficult, remember that there's one person in your life that you tend to treat this way already—you. You "fill the gap with trust" all the time with yourself (even when you probably shouldn't). What we need to do is to extend the same kindness to others.

Assuming the best doesn't mean we put on rose-colored glasses or allow ourselves to be bamboozled. (I've always wanted to use that word in print.) But if our posture is one of trust, we'll approach people with questions rather than accusations. We'll assume there's some information we don't have. As a result, our tone will sound more like, "You aren't usually like this. Is something going on?"[4]

### 3. Promote a culture of grace.

The operative word here is *culture.* That means we interact with the world around us. What they remember about us is not just our firm convictions on truth but the warm way we embraced and accepted them. After all, the Christian life isn't a silo where you only interact with the people who agree with you. Why wouldn't you want the thing they *most* remember about us not just to be the truth we told them but the way we loved them?

Why shouldn't grace characterize all our interactions? This one thing would change the entire tone of the culture war. Grace begets grace.

There's a fascinating example of how grace begets grace, changes the tone, and brings out the best in everybody from Mindy Kaling's (who plays Kelly on *The Office*) book *Is Everyone Hanging Out without Me?* about her time on the cast of *The Office*. In the book she lamented how difficult it was to get Steve Carell (who played Michael Scott) to bad-mouth other cast members—or anyone famous for that matter. She said he exudes a kind of niceness that is so kind and gentle that it's scary.

Kaling says it was her goal throughout the show to get Steve Carell to speak ill of someone else. The cast would be gathered around and invite Carell into the discussion with a look that said, "We're trashing so-and-so to build cast rapport!"[5]

Time after time he just wouldn't engage. He'd smile and politely excuse himself. Kaling couldn't figure out how someone could be—her words—so infuriatingly classy.

I guess Michael Scott got his wish after all:

> *Do I want them to fear me or love me?*
> *I want them to fear how much they love me.*

Carell's actions promoted a culture of grace that impacted the morale of the cast and their chemistry on camera and, thus, the quality of the show—making it one of the most successful sitcoms of all time. I'm on my sixth time through, myself.

As a gospel believer, you should think of yourself as an agent whose mission is to promote grace in every interaction.

So, for instance, when you hear a believer trashing another believer, don't just let it go. Encourage your peers to "fill the gaps with trust." Even if the conflict is about someone you don't even know, you nip it in the bud. You say, "Let's assume that Bill McBillerson is smart and has good intentions" so much that people get sick of hearing it.

You can take this too far, of course. You can become the nosy Trust Police. But most of us are miles away from crossing that line.

A culture of suspicion happens automatically.

A culture of trust takes intentionality.

## 4. Push for direct, honest dialogue.

Tim Challies says that one of the most common phrases pastors should utter after hearing a complaint about someone else is, "Have you spoken to him/her about this?" It can make you feel important to have someone confide in you, but often there is more harm than good in it if they haven't confronted the other person first.

Trust and confrontation aren't opposites.

In fact, each requires the other to exist.

But confrontation, while necessary, has got to be done right—that is, directly, humbly, with an open Bible, open ears, and a humble heart. If we got this right, most of the conflict that plagues our interpersonal relationships would disappear.

## 5. Outdo one another in showing grace.

Proverbs 19:11 says, "It is [a person's] glory to overlook an offense" (ESV). Paul says to the Romans, "Outdo one another in showing honor" (Rom. 12:10 ESV). In this instance Paul is encouraging healthy gospel competition. It's good, he says, to try to be more glorious than your peers in showing grace.

As we've said, there is a time to confront. But there's also a time to make like Elsa and let it go. Wisdom knows when it's time for which.

For some the fear of man may prevent us from confronting others when we ought. For others, arrogance may push us to confront issues that would best be left alone.

Not every battle is worth waging.

Sometimes you gain more ground by losing. And other times you'll lose more ground by winning.

One of my favorite tidbits of counsel from Abraham Lincoln, who was notorious for diffusing conflict and promoting unity, is this:

> No man resolved to make the most of himself
> can spare time for personal contention. Still
> less can he afford to take all the consequences,

including the vitiating of his temper, and the
loss of self-control. Yield larger things to which
you can show no more than equal right; and
yield lesser ones, though clearly your own.
Better give your path to a dog, than be bitten
by him in contesting for the right. Even killing
the dog would not cure the bite.[6]

Sometimes it is better temporarily to lose your spot on the
road than to go home with a dog bite.

Ironically, sometimes the best way to motivate people to be
better is to extend grace to them. Most people want to live up to
the high expectations you hold of them. Sometimes, of course,
you have to sever ties or let someone go. But sometimes gospel
grace is just what they need.

Think of how God changed us: he showed us grace. He
taught us to "renounce ungodliness and worldly passions" by
making the grace of God "appear" to us (Titus 2:8–11 ESV).

We can often compel goodness in people by giving them
grace they don't deserve faster than by giving them the judgment they do deserve.

## MARCHING ORDERS FROM A BIRMINGHAM JAIL

When we dance with this divine tension of grace and truth,
Christianity becomes alive with power. Martin Luther King Jr.
observed in his "Letter from a Birmingham Jail."

There was a time when the church was very
powerful—in the time when the early Christians
rejoiced at being deemed worthy to suffer for
what they believed. In those days the church
was not merely a thermometer that recorded
the ideas and principles of popular opinion;
it was a thermostat that transformed . . . society. . . . Small in number, they were big in commitment. They were too God-intoxicated to be

"[numerically] intimidated." By their effort and example they brought an end to such ancient evils as infanticide and the gladiator games.

Things are different now. . . . And if today's church does not recapture the sacrificial spirit of the early church, it will lose its authenticity, forfeit the loyalty of millions, and be dismissed as an irrelevant social club with no meaning for the twentieth century. Every day I meet young people whose disappointment with the church has turned into outright disgust.[7]

How ironic.

We thought the more we became like the world, the more they would accept us. But the more we became like the world, the more we became irrelevant to them and disgusting to Jesus.

How tragic if the church today forsakes the gospel way in favor of tribalism and power plays.

Remember, truth without grace is judgmental fundamentalism; grace without truth is sentimentality. Combine both and you'll be like Jesus and find yourself attracting people like he did.

People like Rosaria Butterfield.

One last story because this one is personal.

Recently a lesbian couple began attending our church. "Caroline," invited by a friend, attended by herself for a few weeks. God really started to work in her life, and so she convinced her wife, "Jeannie," to come with her.

Jeannie did some research on us.

She learned our convictions about homosexuality and told Caroline, "If you really want to go back to church, that's fine. I'll even go with you. But I'm not going to *that* church."

They did some more research and found a more "affirming" church in our area that was theologically liberal on a number of issues. They had been there three weeks when Caroline looked over at Jeannie and said, "Jeannie, listen, God is not in this church. He was at The Summit Church. We have a choice to make. Either we can come here, where they accept us but God is not present, or we can go to The Summit where God is present and they don't accept our lifestyle. You can do what you want, but I'm going with God."

A few weeks later Caroline gave her life to Christ.

Jeannie struggled for months with Caroline's decision but started to listen to the sermons via podcast. After months she finally worked up the courage to come. Caroline was out of town, so Jeannie came alone, sitting on the second row by herself.

I would not have chosen this for her first week.

Nor, I'm guessing, would she.

I just happened to be in the middle of a series about relationships, and the topic for that week was how God feels about homosexuality and the LGBT community. Do you know how many messages I had preached at The Summit entirely on homosexuality in the last two years?

*One.*

But in God's providence that was the sermon she heard as her "introduction to The Summit Church."

She later told me, "I sat in my pew as mad I had ever been in my life. I decided to take some notes so I could fling some of your statements in Caroline's face and tell her how bad this place was.

"But about ten minutes in I hadn't written anything down.

"I said, '—— it! This is the most loving antigay sermon I've ever heard in my life!'"

A few weeks later Jeannie sat in my office in tears.

She said, "I know it is true. I know that what the Bible says is right, and I am wrong. But I don't know what to do. I want to follow Jesus, like Caroline did, and I'm ready to go wherever he leads."

Caroline and Jeannie are both still works in progress, but their story is one of the most powerful displays of grace I've seen in two decades of ministry.

It's the power of the gospel and nothing more.

This is why we have to make the gospel the center, the focus, the entirety of our ministries. To see more Carolines and Jeannies come to faith in our churches, the gospel has to be above all.

But above *what*, exactly?

Ooh. I'm glad you asked.

Buckle up, the next few chapters could be rough. As my old pastor used to say, "I'm about to go from preachin' to meddlin'."

# CHAPTER 7

# GOSPEL
# ABOVE MY CULTURE

*"Shallow understanding from people of good will
is more frustrating than absolute misunderstanding
from people of ill will. Lukewarm acceptance is
much more bewildering than outright rejection. . . .
In the end, we will remember not the words of our
enemies, but the silence of our friends."*
—Martin Luther King Jr., *The American Civil
Rights Movement 1865–1950*

I never thought "white supremacy" would be a major news item
in the twenty-first century. Maybe that shows how naive I am.
But I legitimately did not think I would have to raise my children in a country that was still battling overt, creedal racism.

And yet, as recently as August 2017,[1] we have seen white
supremacy rear its head—publicly, vocally, violently.

White nationalists organized a march at the University
of Virginia, a march that led to the death of three people and
multiplied a spirit of fear throughout our country. Joe Heim
reported for the *Washington Post*:

> By 8:45 p.m. Friday, a column of about 250 mostly young white males, many wearing khaki pants and white polo shirts, began to stretch across the shadowy Nameless Field, a large expanse of grass behind Memorial Gymnasium at the University of Virginia. Their torches, filled with kerosene by workers at a nearby table, were still dark.
>
> "Stay in formation!" barked an organizer carrying a bullhorn. "Two by two! Two by two!"
>
> Within minutes, marchers lit their torches. Additional organizers, wearing earpieces and carrying radios, ran up and down the line shouting directions.
>
> "Now! Now! Go!"[2]

My wife is a UVA graduate, and I've been on that campus dozens of times.

As I watched the news reports, I recognized the streets of Charlottesville. I remembered specific moments my wife and I had there. Grabbing coffee. Having dinner. Walks through campus and downtown. Good times.

Yet what I saw on the news didn't elicit the same emotions as those emotions.

I was dumbfounded, trying to imagine the spot of my tranquil memories invaded by an angry racist mob. It just didn't make sense.

It shouldn't.

When we hear about tragedies like that of Charlottesville, it's good and right that we respond with unflinching clarity:

> *The spirit of white supremacy is completely antithetical to the gospel.*

I'm shocked that we even need to say this, but as long as the world asks, we need to answer. Those of us who believe the gospel will always oppose ideas that relegate others to any kind of subhuman class. There's only one race of people: human. Only one model of man: the image of God. If we believe the gospel, we always have to resist all forms of racism because to fail to do so is an assault on the God behind our gospel.

I worry, however, that there's a more subtle danger for many of us. Once we've decried the tenets of racism, we think we're off the hook. *Have I ever marched at night, torch in hand, for a white supremacy rally? Absolutely not! Do I make racial slurs? Nope. I must not be the problem then.*

But what if the problem is bigger than the images we're seeing in the news?

Perhaps our problem is deeper than overt racism. Perhaps our real problem is a lack of empathy that dulls our hearts to the burdens borne by other Christians, a lack of charity that makes us question their motives, a lack of trust that belittles their emotions, and a selfishness that makes us unwilling to surrender our privileges and preferences to make "the outsider" feel welcome.

> **Those of us who believe the gospel will always oppose ideas that relegate others to any kind of subhuman class.**

The Scottish preacher Robert Murray McCheyne once wrote, "The seed of every sin is in every human heart." I start my reflection on this with the assumption that the pride that leads to racism, the suspicion that leads to hostility, and the selfishness that refuses to share privilege are endemic to my heart.

I want to suggest that in our day one of the most relevant and countercultural manifestations of gospel power will be multicultural unity in our churches. Our nation desperately wants to see racial unity. But only the gospel has the power to achieve it.

*(Note: While pursuing cultural diversity involves much more than Anglo and African Americans, I am giving special focus to that dynamic here. Much has been written—profitably so—about ethnic diversity among Native Americans, Latinos, East Asians, Arabs, etc. In our nation,*

*though, and in my community, ethnic tension is felt most tangibly in the interactions between white and black Americans—and this is where our church has most tangibly wrestled with it. So it will be the context for much of what I share.)*

## WHAT ELECTION 2016 REVEALED

In theory few people in the American church are opposed to the ideas of racial reconciliation or cultural diversity. But experience would suggest that on this issue good intentions do not equal forward progress.

In fact, a number of recent articles portend even more difficult days ahead.

A 2018 article in the *New York Times*, for instance, described: Once hopeful about the prospects of racial reconciliation, many believers of color—those who were bold enough to enter "white church" settings as pioneers—have grown disheartened and weary by the lack of progress, silently slipping out to rejoin congregations more comfortable for them.[3]

> **Our nation desperately wants to see racial unity. But only the gospel has the power to achieve it.**

Others have not returned to church at all.

Many of these people—and the writer of the *Times* article, too—point to the 2016 presidential election as a milestone moment.

By and large, African American Christians were dismayed at the seeming support evangelicals gave Mr. Trump, despite his persistent moral failures and his troubling comments on issues of race (among other things). It's true, as it has been in many recent general elections, that white and black Christians vote differently. In an oft-cited statistic, among white evangelicals 81 percent voted for President Trump, while 88 percent of churchgoing African Americans voted for Hillary Clinton.

In the dialogues I saw throughout 2016, it was clear that neither side could understand the other. The overwhelming sentiment, from both sides, often boiled down to, *"How could you call yourself a Christian and vote for someone who . . . ?"*

The purpose of this chapter is not to analyze which side made the better argument. As I noted before, the political choices of 2016 were uniquely messy. Many deplored the moral shortcomings of Donald Trump but felt that the alternative was worse. Others, by contrast, felt that voting for Mr. Trump, even reluctantly, was tantamount to a deal with the devil. Trading morality for power.

It's an important discussion, but my point in this chapter is not to make a statement about who was right or wrong.

Instead, I want to point out that Election 2016 revealed something.

*It revealed a divide that has existed for generations.*

This election didn't create it; it only illuminated it.

White evangelicals should have been the first to listen to the fears and frustrations of their African American brothers and sisters. Why didn't we? And black evangelicals should lead in giving their white brothers and sisters the benefit of the doubt wherever they can.

But instead of showing the world a "more excellent way," the church accepted the political and racial battle lines our society was giving us.

In their revelatory book *Divided by Faith,* authors Christian Smith and Michael Emerson conducted a poll of black and white respondents to see what each felt was to blame for disparities in personal accomplishment in our society. In other words, if someone *doesn't* succeed in our society, what, or who, is to blame?

Possible answers could land along a spectrum from individual responsibility on one side to structural bias on the other. This is oversimplified, but it helped me to conceptualize this along a spectrum, something like this:

**Individual Responsibility----- x -------------**
**---- y ------------------ z ----- Systemic Bias**

Person "x" would be more likely to say that the issues lead-ing to poverty are brought on by choices individuals make. *Not studying in school. Not showing up for your job. Not managing money wisely.* Systemic racism, this person believes, is not a major fac-tor; the solution lies mostly with those *in* poverty to work their way out.

Person "z" thinks differently. They see strong systemic forces in play. *How hard a particular person tries has less impact on progress than the systemic biases either for or against them.* Because money is handed down along family lines and shared between people of similar race and background, money tends to stay in the hands of the wealthy and out of the hands of the poor, regardless of work ethic. Lenders are quicker to lend to those of their own ethnic background.

Person "y" represents a median position, in which equal measures of individual and structural issues are involved.

The results of the survey were telling: White Americans tend to explain persistent poverty more along the lines of indi-vidual responsibility, while black Americans believed structural problems are more to blame. The divergence was marked but not as extreme as we might expect. On this chart W stands for "white Americans" and B stands for "black Americans."

**Individual -------------------- W --------------**
**----------- B -------------------- Structural**

Within the church, however, that difference of opinion was even more pronounced. You might visualize it like this, with WC representing "white Christians" and BC standing for "black Christians":

**Individual ---------- WC -------- W ----------**
**---------- B --------- BC ---------- Structural**

The point of all this isn't to tell you which spot on that spectrum is the correct one. That, of course, is an important conversation—but not one we'll have here. The point is to open our eyes to the distance that stands between many black and white Christians today. The perception of where we are, how we got here, and why we stay here is different among white and black Christians. When perceptions are that far apart, we only have one option if we care about bridging the gap.

Listening.

If you are white, for example, don't you want to know *why* your black brothers and sisters so overwhelmingly answer that question the way they do?

I didn't say you will automatically agree with everything they say, any more than I would expect they will agree with whatever you say.

But the apostle Paul wrote, "Carry one another's burdens; in this way you will fulfill the law of Christ" (Gal. 6:2). Part of being one body in Christ is being committed to feeling—and seeking to understand—the pain others are going through.

That starts with listening.

The famous psychologist M. Scott Peck said, "To listen to someone is to love them."[4]

To know someone deeply has to include knowing what has hurt them deeply. Bearing one another's burdens begins with listening and ends with fighting against injustices our brothers and sisters in Christ are experiencing with as much fervency as if they were happening to us or our children.

## WHERE HAVE WE BEEN? RACIAL INJUSTICE IN AMERICA'S PAST

I have always been attracted to the idea of America.

Ours is a nation founded not on ethnic identity but on a creed. In fact, the creed upon which our nation rests is one of equality for all. In many ways the opportunities and freedoms present in our country are unprecedented.

Sadly, many in our country were long kept from those opportunities and freedoms.

Turns out, "equality for all" meant different things for different people. The founders wrote about the equality of all men. And yet these same men saw no problem keeping *other human beings* as property.

As Martin Luther King Jr. often pointed out, our national history has shown that we fail to live up to our own founding creed—with devastating consequences. Here are just a handful of examples:

- **Slavery.** Historically speaking, we are not far removed from the horrific reality of human beings being considered legal—and subhuman—property. Slavery was the status quo in the U.S. from 1619 until 1865—a staggering 246 years.
- **The Three-Fifths Compromise**, which used black slaves for political power (without giving *them* any political power).
- **Sharecropping**, a post-Civil War practice that kept black farmers intractably indebted to wealthy whites.
- **Jim Crow Laws**, which codified segregation, relegating African Americans in substandard schools, restaurants, and transportation.
- **Lynching**, the practice of killing black citizens, which led to the death of thousands and terrorized the entire black community—often with approval from local law enforcement and government officials.
- **Redlining**, in which black neighborhoods were systematically devalued, turning them into urban ghettos.
- **Planned Parenthood**, which was founded on the belief that the minority

population—referred to as "human weeds"—
should be controlled through the targeted
promotion of abortion.

Understanding racial injustice in our nation's past is one of
the key ways we can listen to the voice of our minority brothers
and sisters. As William Faulkner once wrote, "The past is never
dead. It's not even past."

The trauma from yesterday's past is present in today's
tensions.

### The Church's Role in America's Past

In our retelling of history, I've noticed that the church
is usually painted as the "good guy" or the "bad guy." Some
people want to absolve the church of ever having done wrong,
while others seem intent on bashing the faith at every turn.

The reality is somewhere in the middle.

True, Christian doctrine and Bible-thumping Christian
preachers were behind both abolition and the civil rights movements. But we should recognize that, on the whole, many of our
forebears sat in positions of privilege and were blind to injustice.
Many others even actively fought against these movements.

Blindness to evil leads to complicity in evil, so if we are
going to overcome the sins that plague our past and shape our
present, we must look them in the eye.

For those of us in the Southern Baptist Convention (SBC),
the history of injustice in our nation's past is particularly relevant. The SBC was formed in 1845 when American Baptists
split into two factions—those willing to appoint slaveholders as
missionaries (in the South) and those unwilling to do so (in the
North). Unable to reach a consensus, the southern and northern
Baptists split into completely distinct groups.

It is a bit too simplistic to say that the SBC was formed to
defend slavery, but no one denies that slavery was the issue
that split our denomination. Tragically, many early leaders
of the SBC even tried to build biblical defenses of slavery and

segregation in the South. As Southern Baptist Theological Seminary president Al Mohler puts it:

> We cannot tell the story of the Southern Baptist Convention without starting with slavery. In fact, the SBC was not only founded by slaveholders; it was founded by men who held to the ideology of racial superiority and who bathed that ideology in scandalous theological argument.[5]

Now, thank God, the SBC has made clear through a number of formal statements (that go back to the early twentieth century) that we are categorically opposed to slavery and all forms of discrimination and racism. In more recent years the SBC issued a formal apology for their complicity in slavery and segregation (1995). Those statements are an important start, but we are right to be ashamed of how long they took. Because of our denomination's slowness to acknowledge past problems, many African Americans still feel uncomfortable in the SBC.

They have a right to feel that way.

We must also understand that the difficult racial history of the SBC was not merely a matter of origins. Throughout the twentieth century the SBC had a rocky relationship with the civil rights movement. Yes, many of the voices in the civil rights movement were Christian. And many of the SBC resolutions in the 1960s called for an end to racial injustice. But support in the average congregation was often lackluster.

At times even hostile.

Far too often, white conservative Christians—especially in the South—failed to step up. Some leaders, like W. A. Criswell, a kind of SBC godfather, were vocally opposed to the 1956 ruling of *Brown v. Board of Education* (a decision he later called one of the worst mistakes of his life). Most of our forefathers in the faith were more hands off, hiding behind lines like, "Let's not get political" or "Let's just focus on the gospel." Whether they were in support of the civil rights movement or not, they remained largely passive.

I am beginning to see, more and more, just how painful this passivity was to our brothers and sisters of color. Edmund Burke once said that the only thing necessary for evil to triumph is for good men to do nothing. In large measure that's what happened among conservative white Christians fifty years ago.

Here's how Dr. King lamented the situation in his landmark "Letter from a Birmingham Jail":

> I must confess that over the past few years I have been gravely disappointed with the white moderate. [By this he meant white people who chose not to engage.] I have almost reached the regrettable conclusion that the Negro's great stumbling block in his stride toward freedom is not the . . . Ku Klux Klanner, but the white moderate, who is more devoted to "order" than to justice; who prefers a negative peace which is the absence of tension to a positive peace which is the presence of justice; who constantly says: "I agree with you in the goal you seek, but I cannot agree with your methods of direct action"; who paternalistically believes he can set the timetable for another man's freedom; who lives by a mythical concept of time and who constantly advises the Negro to wait for a "more convenient season."[6]

Shallow understanding from people of good will is more frustrating than absolute misunderstanding from people of ill will. Lukewarm acceptance is much more bewildering than outright rejection.

As Pastor Charlie Dates said in 2018 at the "MLK50 Conference: Gospel Reflections from the Mountaintop," believers of color wanted their white brothers and sisters to call out the injustice around them. They wanted to stand united in rebuking a wayward culture.

Instead, they found silence and cultural accommodation.

Pastor Charlie's words reminded me of Dr. King's haunting words: "In the end, we will remember not the words of our enemies, but the silence of our friends."

None of us were around when the SBC split away and became its own denomination in 1845. And few of us were around in the 1950s and '60s, when the people of the SBC were, by and large, strangely silent on issue of racial injustice.

We cannot repent for them.

But we can repudiate their silence.

We can lament the pain these memories cause.

We can commit ourselves not to repeat their errors.

With our brothers and sisters of color, we can ask what we might do to help rectify them.

And as those who continue in the same stream of the SBC, we must do everything we can to remove every last hint of inequity created by the sins of the past.

> Lukewarm acceptance is much more bewildering than outright rejection.

## THE CHURCH'S ROLE IN A "RACIALIZED" SOCIETY

Many people hear about the racial injustices in our nation's past and respond with, "That really was atrocious. And thank God that's in our past. But dwelling on all of that isn't helpful, and it's time we move on."

Well, for one thing, it's easy for those of us in the majority culture to say that. These sins did not affect our ancestors like they did those of our brothers and sisters of color. Furthermore, the long shadow of racism in history impacts our nation's present in profound ways, ways which usually affect communities of color much more adversely than those of the majority. The specter of racism is not so easily exorcised. Sometimes those effects are direct and other times indirect. Our present continues to reverberate with the actions and ideas of our past.

One of the phrases I have found most helpful in thinking about racial issues *today* comes from an African American Christian sociologist George Yancey, professor at North Texas University. He says that despite all our progress on racial issues, we live in a "racialized" society. By that he means that race still has a major effect on many aspects of our lives.

As proof Dr. Yancey points to neighborhoods. Some neighborhoods in the United States are more diverse than others. But it is still incredibly common to have black neighborhoods, Latino neighborhoods, or other pockets of our communities in which one ethnic group predominates. We might shrug this off, but keep in mind that not every social demographic acts this way. We don't have tall neighborhoods or skinny neighborhoods or smart neighborhoods. Those demographic distinctions aren't as critical to our society as ethnic ones.

And our living arrangements show it.

What about the gospel being above all?

If it is true that our society is still heavily influenced by race (i.e., "it's still racialized"), then it should not surprise us that racism still exists.

Now at this point I know many people begin to object. They point out that our laws are much different now than a century ago, or even a generation ago.

Racism hasn't been completely eradicated, but the problem has been *mostly* solved, right? After all, the societal stigma against racism is intense. Can you imagine a worse label than being called "racist"? So certainly the work against racism is just about complete. It's time to move on and not reopen old wounds.

This is where our understanding of history helps us.

When we see the broad strokes of racism in our past, we cannot avoid seeing how racism has deeply impacted social realities like families, governments, and schools. Social realities are slow to change, and while laws are good, they cannot immediately overcome generations of unjust practices.

We see this reality play out when news hits of a white police officer shooting and killing a person of color.

On one side African Americans are keenly aware of racial injustice in our history, so they sense enough of a pattern to assume injustice in *this* particular case. This *one* incident calls to mind not only the long period of public lynchings and other instances of racial violence but their personal encounters and experiences of being racially profiled.

This is a valid viewpoint.

On the other side white commentators often respond by counseling patience. The historical realities may create a disturbing pattern, but it would be unjust to assume the guilt of any individual—white or black—without letting our justice system first pursue the facts. And that is also a valid viewpoint. "Innocent until proven guilty" is a precious and foundational truth in our understanding of justice.

I asked Dr. Yancey about these situations.

"What do you do in a moment like this? It seems we're being asked to choose between two responses, both of which are bringing in strong (and seemingly contrary) assumptions. How do we speak in a way that communicates sympathy without subverting the justice system? I don't want to commit one injustice (depriving the police officer the presumption of innocence and due processes of law) in order to rectify another."

Dr. Yancey responded, "You can always—and should always—come out quickly with sympathy for the victims. After all, it is a tragedy when *anyone* is shot and killed. But you can go further, lamenting the fact that we *still* live in a racialized society whose past makes questions like this even pertinent. It should be unthinkable that ethnicity plays a role in police shootings.

"But it's not. And *that's* a tragedy."[7]

Dr. Yancey is right.

If, God forbid, my white son was shot by the police, I would never ask if his death had anything to do with his skin color.

My African American friends should have that same privilege.

It's past time we ceased thinking about this as a conservative or liberal issue.

The dividing line on this issue is not between conservatives and liberals.

The dividing line runs between those who care about the problem and those who don't.

If the gospel is above all, we will desire a church that reflects the diversity of our communities and proclaims the diversity of the kingdom. If the gospel is above all for us, we will care about this discussion.

## WHERE ARE WE GOING? DECLARING THE DIVERSITY OF THE KINGDOM

*How does the gospel help us move forward from all of this?*

I firmly believe that the best resources for pursuing reconciliation and diversity are found in the depths of the gospel. This is precisely where we need to dig down into the deep caves of gospel resources.

God has declared that diversity is his intention for the church, and he has given his Spirit with the promise that he will make it happen (Eph. 3:1–13; 4:4–5). That's a promise to hold onto even while our society rages in turmoil.

Ethnic diversity is not primarily a worthy *goal* that we pursue. It is a *reality* that God has declared over us in Christ.

> Ethnic diversity is not primarily a worthy *goal* that we pursue. It is a *reality* that God has declared over us in Christ.

Multicultural harmony was one of the distinguishing marks of gospel proclamation in the ancient world, and the unifying power of the gospel hasn't faded.

At The Summit, we have found many of our efforts here guided by the plumb line, "The church should reflect the diversity of its community and declare the diversity of the kingdom." Unity across race and ethnicity is one of the hallmarks of the gospel, a sign to the world that the gospel has real power (Ephesians 2). Our congregations should give evidence to a unity that goes beyond a shared ethnic, cultural, or sociopolitical heritage.

The gospel is for the Jew.

The gospel is for the Greek.

The gospel is for majority culture.

The gospel is for minority culture.

The gospel points to divine unity because we all have the same problem.

We are sinners.

And yet even in that, Paul tells us in Romans, Christ still gave himself for the ungodly. We may all be sinners, but in Christ we are also all equally saved.

Gospel unity is a sign—a preview—of the coming kingdom, in which *every* tribe, tongue, language, and nation will gather around Christ's throne in all their resplendent cultural distinctives (Rev. 5).

Without Christ no one is righteous—not one person.

It is not the color of your skin that welcomes you into God's family; it is the color of crimson-stained wood on Calvary.

You see, Jesus came to inaugurate a new bloodline of relatives, an all-new family connected by means of his sacrificial death and life-restoring resurrection.

That's you. That's me. That's his church.

Through his sacrifice in our place to achieve our adoption, Jesus has eternally altered the DNA of all of God's children. Jesus brings us together in a familial way that we could never have accomplished on our own.

Our new family is not about the bloodline of our ancestors.

It's about the bloodline that began at the cross.

That's the blood that flows through God's family.

That's the bond of the church.

But our journey toward this goal hasn't been easy. True diversity never is. We've learned that diversity isn't a niche "project" for a select few; rather, it is an essential part of discipleship and the responsibility of every follower of Jesus.

For those of us in the majority culture, this process has to begin with a posture of listening, not talking. The definition of a blind spot, after all, is a weakness *we don't know we have.*

We can't see it.

Historically, the most insidious blind spots result from positions of privilege and power. That's not a "white" thing; it's a "people" thing. If we are serious about discovering these blind spots, it means committing ourselves to uncomfortable conversations where we seek more to *understand* than we do to *be understood.*

Not only will we find the experience of listening uncomfortable; we will also likely find that some of the changes necessary to reflect the diversity of the body of Christ will be uncomfortable, too. If we want the church to be a homogenous, white movement, then cultural hegemony is fine. But if we want to reach the diversity of communities throughout the United States, then we better get ready to see our cultural and leadership structures change.

*None of this implies that we need to change any of our doctrine or our core commitments.* Why would it?

If anything, it means we need to press more into them.

It means that a commitment to diversity has to go beyond mere words.

It means that we must reflect on whether the gospel is truly taking root in our churches.

We have to be willing to press through some of the discomfort diversity brings. We have to be willing to second our preferences to those required to reach those who aren't like us.

My friend Vance Pitman models this in his Las Vegas-based church well. He says:

The way to know you are part of a multi-cultural movement is that you at times feel uncomfortable. If you always feel comfortable in your church, then it's probably not multi-cultural, but multi-colored—a group of (mostly) white Southerners who expect those of differing backgrounds to reflect white, Southern culture. Most Southern Baptists seem to want to be a part of a multicolored denomination, not a multi-cultural one.[8]

Our African American brothers and sisters have, for years, been pressing through the discomfort of cultural variances. It is time we in the majority culture join them in that effort.

At The Summit we are constantly urging our people to "get comfortable being uncomfortable." God has, by his grace, given us real progress in this area. Nearly 20 percent of our church attenders are now nonwhite (up from less than 5 percent less than a decade ago). At least a third of our campus pastors and worship leaders are nonwhite. Hear me—our church still has a long way to go. But we are proof that moving toward diversity is possible in a majority culture-dominated church. And while the specifics will look different depending on your demographic situation, positive changes are possible in your church too.

By God's grace I know our churches can move toward diversity and reconciliation.

What we're seeing happen at The Summit Church proves to me that we can.

And I know the Father God wants it.

Because the Son of God promised it.

Thus, the Spirit of God will accomplish it.

## HOW DO WE GET THERE? AIMING FOR TRUE GOSPEL COMMUNITY

One of the biggest lessons we've learned over the past few years is that awareness of a racialized society—while absolutely vital—isn't by itself enough to make diversity a reality. To illustrate this, one of our African American pastors, Pastor Chris Green, summarized the process of a church becoming racially diverse along a helpful spectrum:

*Ignorance* → *Awareness* → *Intentionality*
→ *Gospel Community*

Most of us grow up in communities where those around us look and think like thus. We aren't willfully spiteful or anything, we just don't know much about people from different backgrounds or the experiences they have had. We tend to fill in the gaps with presuppositions and stereotypes. And we assume everyone experiences society like we experienced it.

Recognizing that not everyone experiences society like we do leads us to the next step along the spectrum—awareness.

This usually happens through a relationship, though it can also happen by watching something on the news or through some personal experience that forces us to challenge our previous stereotypes or worldview. I lived in Southeast Asia for a few years and learned what it was like to be viewed through the lens of fear-based, unfair stereotypes. Later, when I began to get close with brothers and sisters of color, I realized that many of them had gone through things in my hometown that I'd never thought twice about. Awareness is unsettling. It challenges a lot of what we assume is simply "normal."

This is where we declare success too quickly.

Most of us assume the process works like that Chutes and Ladders game where once you land on awareness you automatically slide to gospel community.

Acknowledging your newfound awareness and then retweeting some articles about it to signal that you are on the "good guys' team" is not enough.

**The road from awareness to gospel community has to go through *intentionality*.**

The road from awareness to gospel community has to go through *intentionality.*

Change happens when we develop personal relationships with people from other ethnicities and backgrounds, seek to understand them, learn to respect them, and learn from them. That begins the lifelong quest toward gospel community.

I can't emphasize this enough: multicultural gospel community has got to begin on the relational level.

At our church we say that our goal should not be to host multicultural events but to live multicultural lives. If we live multicultural lives, then multicultural events will happen naturally and authentically. In practice this means we constantly ask ourselves, *Do I have friends who are not like me? Am I seeking to embrace, and learn from, other cultures? Do I have relationships that would make a watching world wonder why we are friends when we seem to have so much that separates us?*

United in Christ, we aren't pursuing *sameness* but a covenant community of *oneness.*

Dr. King famously said that 11:00 on Sunday morning was the most segregated hour in America.

Perhaps there is one exception: 6:00 around the table each evening.

Our dining rooms need diversity just as much as our church gatherings. Until that happens, the diversity in our gatherings will be just a stage show.

## BEGIN AGAIN, PETER

The early church had its own issues with discrimination and privilege. Even Peter, arguably the foremost leader of the church, got caught discriminating against other believers outside of his culture.

So Paul confronted him, he tells us in Galatians, to his face.

Can you imagine being publicly confronted by Paul?

Not a fun day to be Peter.

"You've forgotten the gospel," Paul told him. Bold statement to make to the head of the church, who studied under Jesus directly for the last three years.

In the gospel, Paul reminded him, everything we have is a gift of grace. There is nothing about us that God saw was better than someone else. And if God included us when we were outsiders, Paul asked, how dare we exclude someone else?

Do you really think you are something, Peter? Do you not remember where you were when God saved you?

We came to Jesus full of shame, stains, dirt, believed the gospel, and walked away 100 percent spotless, clean, accepted, and righteous.

Furthermore, the gospel teaches us that Jesus sacrificed all his preferences to enter our world and save us. Why wouldn't we do that for others? Think about it: Can you imagine the cultural differences between heaven and the dirty, backwards community in Nazareth Jesus made his home? But Jesus considered our salvation "more important" than his heavenly comforts, and so he set them all aside and took upon himself the form of a servant so that he could save us (Phil. 2:5–11).

See what I mean about the gospel containing all the power necessary for racial unity?

This is why we as Christians can offer something our society can only yearn for. Our society wants us to be aware. At key moments of national tragedy, they want us to interact. They want to get along. But they can't offer a way for us to love one another like family.

As the old saying goes, the ground is level at the foot of the cross.

Practically, for those of us in church leadership, pursuing gospel community means we structure our services differently than if our entire church were white (we'll talk about that more in the next chapter). It means we prioritize diversity in the leaders we're developing. It means we facilitate conversations where it is safe to talk about ethnic differences and the challenges that result from them. It means we value gospel unity over political alignment (which we'll talk about in chapter 8). It means we lead the way in modeling multicultural friendships.

> **Jesus did not introduce a new religion; he introduced a new humanity.**

This kind of familial unity turned heads when Christianity burst onto the scene in the first century. It showed people that Jesus had not introduced a new religion; he had introduced a new *humanity*. And if we let the gospel transform us so that we live multicultural lives, it's going to turn heads today, too.

## A *KAIROS* MOMENT

I believe the American church is in a *kairos* moment regarding race.

*Kairos* is a Greek word for time that implies a specially appointed moment in history. I believe God has appointed this moment in the world for the church to rise up and demonstrate a unity in Christ for which the world yearns.

What our society has been unable to produce through its laws, God creates through the gospel. It's *that* powerful. *It is* the power of God. That's why it should be above all.

The Bible teaches us about three great common factors all humans share:

All men and women are created equal because they are each alike made in the image of God.

All ethnicities suffer from a common problem—sin.

And all of us look toward a common hope—Jesus.

The gospel creates a new humanity, a redeemed race made up of all colors, in Christ's image.

In fact, here's a little known fact about the book of Romans, Paul's longest-ever treatment of the gospel. It was written to a church experiencing ethnic division between Jew and Gentile. Paul was showing the Romans that through the cross, God had created a brand-new humanity that transcended any divisions they experienced in society.

That means that whenever we experience ethnic strife in our churches, it's probably not because our ethnic differences are too big. It's that our gospel is too small.

God created a diversity of ethnicities to display his glory like a multisplendored diamond, and we ought to see that glory first reflected in the church.

Not only were we created as one race, but around the great throne of Christ in Revelation, we will worship the risen Son as a new redeemed race made up of people from every tribe, tongue, and nation. Thus, as a matter of gospel faithfulness, the church, God's "plan A" for rescuing the world, must stand as a place of refuge for people of every color, a beacon pointing to what is to come.

*Reflect the diversity of the community and proclaim the diversity of the kingdom. The makeup of our attendance on the weekend should unequivocally declare:*

We are one race—human.

With one problem—sin.

United under one Savior—Jesus Christ.

In love with one color—crimson red.

Looking forward to one hope—*resurrection.*

Gospel above all.

# CHAPTER 8

# **GOSPEL** ABOVE MY PREFERENCES

*"If my hearers are not converted, I feel like I have
wasted my time; I have lost the exercise of brain and
heart. I feel as if I lost my hope and lost my life,
unless I find for my Lord some of his blood-bought
ones. . . . I would sooner bring one sinner to Jesus
Christ than unpack all the mysteries of the divine
Word, for salvation is the thing we are to live for."*
–Charles Spurgeon

The woman at the well tried to draw Jesus into a worship war.

"This is how we Samaritans think you should worship," she said.

But Jesus didn't take the bait. At least not fully.

He took her bait and hooked her with it. He told her the Father was seeking *any* who would worship him in spirit and in truth.

She'd never heard of that style.

"Worshipping in truth" means thinking rightly about God. "In spirit" means that our worship has to be more than a head thing. It's a spirit-with-Spirit thing. It's not knowledge only; it's intimacy.

In worship, God wants our minds thinking rightly about the gospel and our spirits responding rightly to the gospel. So, if that's what *God* really cares about, why do we argue so much about what church services are supposed to look like?

Based on Jesus' answer, I can't see him thinking worship is about whether you use guitars. Or handbells. Or drum sets. Or whether you clap. Or use hymnals. Or a fog machine. Or a spoken word. Or four-part harmony with shape notes. Or go for one hour or three.

Worship is right thinking about God and right response to the gospel.

I have the privilege of pastoring at a church where people come from various backgrounds. And with those various backgrounds come differing expectations for a worship service.

We have a lot of traditional Southern Baptists.

There's not a lot of *movement* in their worship, but there's plenty of volume, especially when we bring out the old hymns. If they are really into it, they may lift one arm for a moment like they are trying to ask a question. If they are experiencing revival, they'll sway back and forth with both arms bent 90 degrees at the elbows, as if they're carrying an invisible television.

And of course, they only sing the words that are written in the songs.

When I preach, they'll let out punctuated, staccato "amens" every time I hit an alliterated point.

Mixed in among them is a sizable number of African Americans.

Some in this crowd are a bit more loquacious with their sermon feedback. They like to "help me out" (their words) when I'm preaching—talking back to me in full sentences, with verbs, adverbs, dependent clauses, and occasionally questions. More than once I've wondered if I was supposed to pause and actually *answer* the question or tuck it away for next time.

During worship they match our white members in volume, while adding in a rhythmic clapping, shouting, and jumping I don't typically see from our members that grew up at First Baptist of Old Holler. And some of them sing as many words that *aren't* written in the songs as ones that are.

Our Latino members combine this sanctified enthusiasm with a supernatural endurance. They are genuinely mystified by how we can "do church" in an hour and fifteen minutes. Our Hispanic pastor tells me they are barely through the announcements by then. And anything less than two hours of singing cannot legitimately be called "worship." I'm serious: the first time I attended a service at our Summit en Español campus, I missed lunch with my family. And I think maybe dinner, too.

When it comes to boisterous worship, though, our Korean members are in a class by themselves.

For a while we had a group of Korean students who sat in the second row. The first time I saw them worshipping I honestly thought someone was going to get hurt.

They weren't "singing" the songs.

They were yelling them.

Sometimes stomping with the beat.

Several of them looked like they were trying to give God up in heaven a high five. But when I got up to preach, it was like someone flipped a switch.

Off.

These passionate worshippers became stone silent the entire time I preached, even during the good parts. After this happened several weeks in a row, I was actually a little discouraged. I thought maybe my messages weren't connecting with them, so I finally asked one of them.

"You are so enthusiastic when you're singing. But during the sermons . . ." I struggled to find the right question. "Am I just not making sense to you?"

My friend looked confused for a moment and then said, "Oh, no, Pastor J. D.! We love your preaching as much as we love the music. But in our culture it is impolite to talk when the pastor is speaking. Sitting quietly is how we show respect for you and the Word that is being preached."

So here's our question: Which of these styles is the correct, biblical way to worship?

Well, yes and amen.

I realize I'm generalizing here about white, African American, Latino, and Korean believers, and plenty of exceptions can be found to the above. But the point is that Christians come to church preferring different styles, and often those styles correspond with their cultural upbringing.

## BECOMING A "JEW TO THE JEWS"

For the apostle Paul, the question was not which style of worship he preferred but, "What best helps me reach people with the gospel?" In fact, he said some genuinely startling things about the changes he was willing to make to that end. Listen to what he says to the Corinthians:

> For though I am free from all, I have made myself a servant to all, that I might win more of them. To the Jews I became as a Jew, in order to win Jews. To those under the law I became as one under the law (though not being myself under the law) that I might win those under the law. To those outside the law I became as one outside the law (not being outside the law of God but under the law of Christ) that I might win those outside the law. To the weak I became weak, that I might win the weak. I have become all things to all people, that by all means I might save some. (1 Cor. 9:19–22 ESV)

The most interesting part of this passage to me is Paul's statement that "to the Jew I became like a Jew." Uh . . . Paul *was* a Jew. So how does a Jew become a Jew to reach the Jews? When is a Jew not a Jew? (Ask the question enough times, and you begin to hear a Dr. Seuss book in the making.)

If nothing else, it shows us that Paul held his own Jewish culture *so loosely* that he actually had to *readopt* it in engaging with other Jews. He took it off and on like a garment. A truly gospel-loving Christian will do the same.

That should mean, for example, that I have to rebecome a Southern American when engaging with other Southern Americans. Not because I despise my culture and am trying to distance myself from it but because I recognize that even though my identity in Christ doesn't expunge my culture, it does relativize it (along with every other facet of my being).

Let that marinate in your brainpan for a while.

Or, as some of our African American members would say, "You tell 'em, preacher."

## WHY THE MUSIC MATTERS

We are a few years removed from the famous "worship wars," but it is amazing how divisive musical worship preferences still can be. In the Western world, at least, believers can agree with a church in every major doctrinal question, but if the music isn't right, they feel like they don't fit and will go elsewhere. Sadly it is probably one of the main reasons people either leave our church for another or come to us from a different one.

That's because music and culture are intimately connected.

In fact, I think you can look at musical preferences and how we deal with them as a microcosm for a whole set of cultural preferences. It's often where the "rubber meets the road" in our willingness to engage in multicultural diversity.

Most of us aren't as flexible as we'd like to think.

Early in my ministry I spoke with a white college student who was exhorting me to better integrate minorities into our church. I agreed with everything this young man said, so I was surprised when he popped up after service one weekend with a complaint.

Apparently, he didn't like some of the changes we had been making in worship. He wasn't fond of some of the newer songs we were singing and didn't appreciate that our worship leader was urging people to clap and raise their hands.

Perhaps this college student was not as eager for multicultural worship as he indicated. Perhaps what he really wanted was *multicolored* worship, where people of differing colors all worshipped the way he preferred.

Not the same.

I'd be harder on him if I weren't just like him.

As I mentioned in the last chapter, Vance Pitman says that the sign you are in a multicultural church is that at times you feel uncomfortable. Even if you are the pastor! And in my experience, one of the first areas that discomfort manifests is with the music. If the music in your church never feels uncomfortable to you—well, it does to somebody.

Our problem in this is that we can't understand why people would *not* want to express themselves in worship like we would. We assume their reluctance to worship like us is evidence of some innate spiritual flaw.

For instance, some of the more "expressive" people in our church respond with frustration to the less-expressive believers and wonder how they can remain so unemotional in the presence of so great a God. "You will scream like a maniac *for the sake of a basketball team*," they argue, "so why wouldn't you do it for the God of the universe? Does King James (LeBron James) really deserve a more rousing response than King Jesus?"

On the other side, there are those who feel like emotionally charged worship is manipulative, exploiting crowd dynamics and then labeling all that commotion "the Spirit." Many in our Western context—believers and unbelievers alike—are skeptical of such coerced emotional moments, *especially* when you label those moments "the Spirit of God."

So which culture's concerns are more valid?

As I said before, yes and amen.

Both sides bring truths to the worship conversation that must be heard and heeded.

Is it possible for our worship to be deceitful, contriving emotional moments?

Absolutely.

But is it possible for our worship to be stale and lacking an appropriate enthusiasm, an enthusiasm we freely pour out for other, lesser things?

Absolutely.

We need to stop thinking about worship in our churches as an "either-or" between two diametrically opposed extremes. Like many areas of ministry, this is a place where we live in tension, balancing the "both-and" of mind *and* heart, wisdom *and* passion.

We must study our Bibles, analyze our given contexts, and be open to worshipping together with others who express themselves in different ways than we do.

The gospel calls us to reach more than the people who are *just like us*.

And that means we have to get comfortable feeling uncomfortable.

And along the way we'll probably have some blind spots revealed. That's one of the many beauties of God's multicultural body. We are more complete together than we are apart.

## OPEN HAND OR CLOSED HAND?

A crucial component of this discussion is knowing how to separate "cultural preference" from "scriptural value." On the one hand, some of the Bible's harshest condemnations are reserved for those who couldn't separate these two ideas. Jesus, for instance, blasted the Pharisees of his day for clinging so closely to their traditions that they were actually breaking the law of God:

> "Why do you break God's commandment because of your tradition? For God said: 'Honor your father and your mother'; and, 'Whoever speaks evil of father or mother must be put to death.' But you say, 'Whoever tells his father or mother, "Whatever benefit you might have received from me is a gift committed to the temple," he does not have to honor his father.' In this way, you have nullified the word of God because of your tradition. Hypocrites! Isaiah prophesied correctly about you when he said: 'This people honors me with their lips, but their heart is far from me. They worship me in vain, teaching as doctrines human commands.'" (Matt. 15:3–9)

And then there's Paul, who in the last chapter rebuked the apostle Peter to his face for prioritizing cultural customs over gospel unity (Gal. 2:11–14). Woe to us if we ever say, "Thus says the Lord" about one of our preferences when God hasn't spoken!

Scholars have noted that many of the books of the Old Testament have a counterpart in the New. The Old Testament apocalyptic book of Daniel finds its counterpart in Revelation, for example. Historical books like Exodus or 1–2 Samuel find their counterparts in the historical accounts of the Gospels and Acts. Wisdom literature like the book of Proverbs finds many parallels with the book of James.

But nowhere do we find a counterpart to the book of Psalms, ancient Israel's worship songbook.

I don't think this is an accident.

Certainly the New Testament church had a set of songs they sang, just like the people of Israel did. Part of me wishes they were preserved for history. But mostly I'm thankful the apostles chose *not* to codify a New Testament worship manual.

Why? Because we would have taken *that* musical expression, shaped by *that* one culture, and declared it to be gospel. Even though we put some of the ancient psalms to modern music, they were written originally for Jewish culture, with Yiddish meter and Hebrew rhyme. All music is that way, and if there were a New Testament book of Psalms, that culture's style of worship would be more normative for the church.

Friends, worship in the church was never meant to be shaped by one culture. God left a musical preference out of the New Testament on purpose.

These cultural preferences are all things we should hold with an open hand, ready to alter or remove them as the mission demands. On the other hand, however, are a number of things we must remain closed handed with. The gospel cannot be compromised. Nor should essential doctrine, ethics, purity, integrity, humility, submission to Scripture. These things must go in a closed hand that we refuse to change no matter how great the cultural pressure.

Scripture ought to shape our approach to *all* of ministry, and there is much in the New Testament that prescribes what God desires from our worship. We are not free to worship him however we want. In the Old Testament people died for trying that (Lev. 10:1–3). Corporate worship, for instance, should always be congregational and not regularly be practiced in isolation via a live-stream connection. Preaching must be given a central place in every church, and that preaching must be grounded in the authority and inerrancy of the Bible. Prayer should be an essential element of our gatherings. There must be space for people to exercise their spiritual gifts. The two ordinances, the Lord's Table and baptism, must be observed regularly. And many other things. While the practice of these elements may look different from one church to another, no church ought to neglect any of them. They must remain in the closed hand.

In the open hand are those elements of worship that we can change—the things Paul refers to as "becoming a Jew to the Jews." The tragedy of the evangelical church is that we've swapped our hands, putting things in the wrong hands.

Some churches long ago left behind the centrality of God's Word and the inerrancy of the Bible but fired pastors for attempting to remove the organ from the sanctuary.

Their hands got crossed.

## WHEN JESUS GOT MAD

The maddest we see Jesus get in the Gospels occurs when he observes Jewish leaders cluttering up the court of the Gentiles with conveniences for the saved. He saw that the court had been overrun by peddlers selling sacrifices to be used in temple worship.

Primarily, Jesus was angry that they had consumed the only space set apart for Gentiles to seek God. With the backing of a whip, Jesus exclaimed, "My house was intended to be a house of prayer for all nations, but you have turned it into a den of thieves" (Mark 11:17, author's paraphrase).

Maybe you were taught like I was—that what made Jesus mad was people making money in church. The application was that if you were in going to sell CDs, books, or shirts in the church lobby, they shouldn't be at a large markup. That's probably also valid, but the first part of his statement reveals the source of his anger:

"My house was *designated to be a house of prayer for the nations.*"

This wasn't primarily about his displeasure over selling overpriced T-shirts in our lobbies.

Jesus was angry not only at what they were doing but at what their customs were keeping others from doing. They had transformed the only open-access point for the Gentiles into a catalog of comforts and conveniences for those already saved!

Having a place to change money and buy and sell sacrifices so close to the altar was convenient for believing Jews, of course. Problem was, this kept outsiders out of the one place where they could observe the beauties of worship.

I imagine some of the Jews could have retorted: *"But Jesus, this temple is not primarily for the Gentiles. It's for the Jews. Temple worship is not for the unsaved but the saved."* And technically they would have been correct. But God had also commanded the Jews, as a *part of* their worship, to provide easy access to seeking Gentiles to hear and know truth, and when they didn't, Jesus became furious. They had transformed a portal for the outsider into a convenience store for the insider.

Why would Jesus feel any differently today about a church that makes no accommodations in its preaching, music, language, preferences, practice of traditions, children's programs—even things like parking and signage—to make the gospel accessible to outsiders? By not thinking of the "observing outsiders" whom God is drawing to himself during our worship, are we not creating the same roadblocks for "Gentiles" as the Jews did in Jesus' day?

**How must Jesus feel when a church refuses even to *consider* what needs to change in its traditions if it is to reach the next generation?**

It seems that many churches care more about holding on to their traditions than they do even reaching their grandchildren.

How must Jesus feel when a church refuses even to *consider* what needs to change in its traditions if it is to reach the next generation?

## CHOOSING OUR TRADITIONS OVER OUR GRANDCHILDREN

I know it may sound like I'm hatin' on traditions. I'm really not.

Traditions can be the guardians of wisdom. As G. K. Chesterton once said, if we come upon a gate across a road and are not sure why it is there, removing it before we know who put it up and why may not be the wisest course of action.[1] Observing tradition can be a shortcut to wisdom, a humble response to our forefathers who learned things through trial and error and want to pass on the blessing of their wisdom to us.

On the other hand, as we've seen, Scripture makes clear that we stand condemned if we cannot–or will not–separate our cultural practices from essential gospel truths, thereby creating hindrances to the gospel.

We've got to be candid with ourselves that a lot of our traditions have nothing to do with the gospel. They are merely reflections of our preferences, or our parents' preferences, or our grandparents' preferences. And while we should love our grandparents, we also need to love our grandchildren enough to reach *them* with the gospel.

In the passage from 1 Corinthians 9, noted earlier, where Paul explains what he's willing to do to reach people, he compares the whole process to a race (1 Cor. 9:24). If I'm running a race, whether that race is a 100-meter sprint or a 26.2-mile marathon, I'm not bringing along any excess weight. I may love my fifty-five-volume collection of the complete works of Martin Luther (indeed, it is one of my most prized possessions), but Luther's not coming with me during a marathon.

I'm shedding everything that gets in the way of winning.

Why does this make so much sense for an actual race but feel so difficult in church life? Isn't the race to win people's souls the most urgent race of all?

I think part of the problem is we occupy ourselves so much with what we're *losing* that we don't stop to think of what we're *gaining.* Letting preferences and traditions go is hard. There's no doubt about it. But sacrifice is about more than losing.

Sacrifice means giving up something you love for something you love even more.

I love my traditions and cultural preferences, but I love my lost neighbors more. So I'd gladly give up the former to gain a few more of the latter.

Jesus thought I was worth leaving heaven for. Are my lost neighbors not worth giving up my preferences?

The willingness to change can only be sustained, in the long run, by a passion for the lost. When people begin to ache, like Paul did, for the lost, being willing (as he said he was in Rom. 9:1–3) even to go to hell for them, letting go of their cherished traditions won't seem like such a sacrifice.

I saw that transformation take place nearly two decades ago at The Summit. About a month after I became the pastor, we found a set of handbells in a storage closet. We weren't using them, and no one could even remember the last time we brought them out. Some of you reading right now are asking yourself, "What in the world is a handbell?" YouTube it. Amazing.

Well, we needed some new worship equipment, and they were valuable, so it just made sense to sell them and use the funds to get new stuff.

A few weeks later a sweet lady—whose family had been at our church for years—approached me, telling me she had heard about our plans and asking why we were doing it.

I tried to explain, when she politely interrupted and said, "My mother, who died a few years ago, left the money to purchase those handbells to the church in her will."

There was a long pause.

I panicked. Our plan was to purchase two electric guitars with the money from the sale. I didn't know what to say. I dropped my head and silently began making vows to God.

Somewhere in the distance a dog barked.

I choked out our plans.

She said, "My mother's endowment is being used to purchase electric guitars?"

Searching for something, I said to her, "Well, don't you think your mom in heaven would be glad to see us using instruments that would help us reach this next generation—including her grandkids and their friends?"

She thought about that for a second, and then smiled and said, "Well, yes . . . I suppose my mom would be happy with that. That's a good way to think about it."

This kind lady then requested that we not sell the handbells but donate them instead to another church. And I was glad to make that compromise. Yet she did not resist seeing them go, and she has not left our church as we have tweaked our worship style numerous times in attempts to reach new generations and new communities. She's still in our church today, every week lifting her hands in worship led by guitars and keyboards instead of the handbells she had loved.

And thousands of college students join her. Because of her selflessness, our church is reaching a whole new generation.

Am I saying that a church needs guitars to reach the next generation? Not exactly. In fact, some churches even find that younger people are attracted to more traditional, liturgical styles of worship. How this plays out at your church may look different than it does ours. But the core idea *has* to be there: if our worship style forces us to choose between reaching our grandchildren and clinging to our traditions, I'm choosing the grandkids every time.

Somewhere around that same time, I had the privilege of baptizing a young man named Antwain. As far as I knew, Antwain was the first African American we had ever baptized at The Summit. His story was incredible. He had endured a difficult past, to put it mildly. We met at an "open gym" night I hosted in our church's gymnasium. His nickname was "Air" because of how high he could jump. (Everyone had nicknames. One guy was called "Money" because he rarely missed a three pointer; another was called "Butter" because of how well he could drive the ball. I was called "No, Don't Shoot." True story.)

After several months of friendship with Antwain, long talks, dinners, and Bible study, the light of grace finally broke through, and I was there with him as he prayed to receive Christ.

He stood in our baptistery a few Sundays after that and gave one of the clearest testimonies to Christ's power I'd ever heard. It was amazing, and there was scarcely a dry eye in the house when he was finished. And then I baptized him.

After the service an older gentleman in our church approached me.

"Son," he said, "you know I don't like a lot of these changes you are making in our church."

I worried about where this conversation was going. I stood there quietly. Pretty sure that same dog barked somewhere in the distance again.

Then he got choked up and said, "But if that right there is what we're getting, you can count me in for all of them."

This is the heart of those who put the gospel above their preferences.

## MAKING IT HARD FOR GENTILES TO GET TO GOD

A few years ago I was preaching through the book of Acts when a phrase seemed to jump off the page at me. It was James's conclusion to a really difficult discussion about which of the Jewish traditions they were going to insist the newly believing Gentiles ought to keep so there could be harmony in the church:

> It is my judgment, therefore, that we should not make it difficult for the Gentiles who are turning to God. (Acts 15:19 NIV)

Another Bible teacher said about that phrase,

> If I could, I would write this on the pulpit of every church in America. I would engrave that phrase into the cornerstone of every church.

I think about this phrase sometimes when I am preaching. And sometimes when we are making decisions about which worship styles to employ, which church programs to pursue, or which rules and standards to require. I think about it when election time rolls around, and I'm deciding whether to put a sign in my yard or a bumper sticker on my car.

I never want to shy away from preaching a single truth from Scripture, *but I also do not want to make it difficult for people unfamiliar with Christianity to turn to God.* I do not want to make it difficult for guests drawn to our church who have heard God is at work here—but then they get here and parking is horrendous, the kids' rooms are overcrowded, and the worship area is messy. I don't want people to turn away from our church because we didn't think ahead to have enough volunteers to welcome them.

I do not want to make it difficult for people trying to get into discipleship by having a process too cumbersome to figure out.

I do not want to make it difficult for the de-churched to turn *back* to God because I use Christianese when I preach or caricature unbelievers in ways that lampoon and mischaracterize their opinions, showing I don't really respect them.

I do not want to make it difficult for someone to turn back to God because I have a sign in my yard supporting a candidate they don't like.

I do not want to make it difficult for people of other ethnicities that are turning to God because we have no multicultural representation in our leadership or because we are tone-deaf to their concerns.

I do not want to make it difficult for those struggling with same-sex attraction who are turning to God by stigmatizing that sin, treating it as categorically different from my own, or by failing to treat them as individuals made in the image of God who are often confused and hurting. A friend of mine says that every teenager who left the church because of a same-sex attraction was first a person in our churches who couldn't understand why God would not answer their prayer to take this attraction away. I want to speak with clarity about this issue—homosexual behavior is sin—but also with tenderness and compassion. Gay, lesbian, and transgender people are first and foremost people made in the image of God. They're not defined by their sexual identity but by the one in whose image they are made. They should mainly feel from me the respect and compassion that goes with that, not that they are the objects of my derision or scorn or a voting bloc to be marginalized.

If Christianity is offensive, I want to let the gospel do the offending, not me.

Grace and truth.

Shouldn't any person who has tasted of the unmerited generosity of the gospel do everything they can to remove the obstacles between their neighbors and God?

How could we worship a Savior who left everything to make a way for us and not be willing to lay aside our preferences and conveniences for them?

## OUT OF OUR MINDS . . . FOR THEM

I heard a story years ago about an earthquake that happened in California.

A man was being interviewed who had been driving late one night, around 3:00 a.m., when the earthquake hit. He pulled over, he said, waited for the earthquake to stop, and then slowly pulled back on to the road. Despite the sudden surprise of the event, he seemed none the worse for wear.

Until he noticed the taillights of the car in front of him suddenly disappear.

He slowed down, and as he approached the spot where the lights had disappeared, he slammed on his brakes. The taillights had disappeared because the car had plunged over the edge of a cliff. The earthquake, it seemed, had completely taken out this small highway bridge.

Peering over the edge of the cliff, he saw the car, demolished, in the ravine below. But as he considered what he might do to help, he turned around to see more cars headed toward him.

He waved his hands and screamed for the first car to stop. The driver ignored him.

(After all, would *you* have stopped at 3:00 a.m. if a stranger on the side of the road was screaming at you?) The man watched, in horror, as the car disappeared over the edge of the cliff. He had no more luck with the second car, which ignored him and plunged into the ravine.

And that's when he saw a bus coming around the corner.

"At that moment," he said, "I resolved that the only way that bus was going over the cliff was if it was taking me with it."

He moved into the middle of the road.

Waving his shirt and screaming like a madman, he yelled, "Stop! Stop! Stop!" Fortunately, the bus stopped. And while the bus driver jumped out of the bus initially furious, when he saw what had happened—and realized how many lives this man had saved—he was immensely grateful.

When I heard that story, I thought, *What would I have done if I were there?* I hope I would have done the same thing that man did—acting like I was *out of my mind* for the sake of saving lives. Would I have cared that the people driving by thought I was acting like a lunatic? Of course not.

Because I had seen something they hadn't.

How much more, when it comes to the gospel, should we be willing to be—in the words of the apostle Paul—a madman for the sake of Christ (2 Cor. 5:13)? Should we not be willing to say, "I've seen something you haven't seen, and I'm pleading with you to listen"? Sharing the gospel is an urgent rescue mission, more urgent than if we'd seen a bus full of people hurtling toward a cliff.

It's time we stop playing church and start realizing what's at stake.

Every day thousands of people hurtle into an eternity without God. It's a fate astronomically worse than crashing into a ravine. That fact requires an urgency among those of us who believe. It requires an urgency that others might consider over the top. It requires an urgency that makes us willing to lay aside our preferences, even our cultures. To lay them aside like a jacket on a hot day.

How can we honestly say we're a gospel people if the handbells—or the electric guitars—are so important to us that we'll let them keep people from hearing the gospel? How can we say we're a gospel people if we're so married to our preferences that we'll prevent who-knows-how-many "Gentiles" from ever once hearing the good news of Jesus?

Could it be that the reason people don't believe in the urgency of the gospel is because we don't show that urgency in the way we share it? Because we value our own personal preferences and opinions more than their eternities?

Shouldn't we again become those people who stand in the middle of the road, waving our shirts, calling people to flee to Christ for salvation?

# CHAPTER 9

# GOSPEL
# ABOVE MY POLITICS

*"Christian political engagement is an endlessly
difficult subject. Our Lord said to render to Caesar
what is Caesar's and to God what is God's, but he
did not accommodate us by spelling out the details.
For over two thousand years, Christians have again
and again thought they got the mix just right, only to
have it blow up in their faces. We're always having
to go back to the drawing board, which is to say, to
first things. Even when, especially when, we are most
intensely engaged in the battle, first things must be
kept first in mind. . . . It profits us nothing if we win
all the political battles while losing our own souls."*
–Richard John Neuhaus

"I hope you get cancer and die, you _____."

I generally consider my memory to be rather average.
Perhaps less than average. But I'll probably remember every
word of that little jab for the rest of my life.

I don't often receive vitriol like this, but when I do, it typically comes after something I've said gets construed as political.

Perhaps you can relate. Post a photo of your dinner on Facebook, and you probably won't ruffle many feathers. Share your views about politics—however nuanced, gracious, and balanced, and no matter the view—and your comment stream is likely to turn into a digital version of the profane scribbles on a bathroom stall. Engaging with the comments under your political post is like wrestling with a pig in the mud. You both end up dirty, but the pig liked it.

Politics has never been an arena that warms the heart, but it seems a particularly treacherous topic today. It's kind of like a skunk. Touch it, and it's all you'll smell like for a month.

If I were to mention a political position one time out of a hundred sermons, chances are that's the only thing I'd be known for in the public eye. It wouldn't matter how many other sermons I preached.

The question of politics has always been a tough one for me personally.

I went to college to major in political science with plans to go to law school and become a politician.

On one hand, I believe Christian truth permeates every arena of life. As Abraham Kuyper, the Dutch prime minister of the early twentieth century, said, "There is not a square inch in the whole domain of our human existence over which Christ, who is Sovereign over all, does not cry, 'Mine!'"[1]

That means Christians should bring divinely informed wisdom into questions of taxation, Medicare, racial justice, global warming, and literally every other area of public life. Because Christians got involved in the early days of American history, for example, we have things like freedom of speech, freedom of religion, and a host of other political blessings. Thank God for them.

But because they *didn't* get appropriately involved in the 1960s, the civil rights movement was much harder and much slower than it needed to be.

On the other hand, "touching the skunk" might permanently obscure our gospel aroma in the nostrils of many.

As Christians, it's easy to look at politics and want to walk away altogether, *especially* in recent years. It's much harder—and much more necessary—to engage in politics as one way of impacting our society, and to do so in a manner that keeps the gospel fixed firmly in its rightful place.

If the gospel is above all, what does that mean for political engagement?

It can't mean that we cease engaging altogether because Jesus commanded us to be salt and light in our communities, to give unto Caesar what is Caesar's, to be a blessing to our cities, and to never cease fighting for truth, justice, and compassion. That requires engagement in politics.

But how can we do so in a way that shows that our primary commitment is not to a party or to a platform but to the gospel?

How do we engage in a way that ultimately shows we believe salvation does not come riding in on the back of a donkey or an elephant but cradled in a manger—and that the animal you vote for is not as important as the Savior you worship?

How do we engage in a way that shows redemption is found not in the stars and stripes of our flag but the scars and stripes on our Savior?

## THE FOUR MYTHS

I've found that there are four major myths Christians tend to believe when it comes to the gospel and politics. To put the gospel above all means avoiding all four of these.

### Myth 1: The gospel doesn't apply to politics.

As I mentioned, the freedoms we enjoy as a nation don't stand as isolated ideals. Many arose as believers applied biblical truth to the public square. Some are so commonly accepted now that we forget how unheard of they were until Christians presented them as civic ideals. Furthermore, our nation's earliest hospitals, institutions of higher learning, and education systems were all built by Christians. Christians pioneered nearly every "helping profession," including nursing and social work. Further back still, Christians were the only ones opposing accepted cultural practices like infanticide and child abuse, arguing that *every* person was worthy of dignity and honor.

In short, nothing is more logical and reasonable than Christianity bearing fruit in the public square.

And that's something our society still needs from us.

As the African American economist from Stanford, Thomas Sowell notes, the Christian worldview teaches distinctive truths about the nature of man, the value of life, the principles of justice, and the dangers of power. Other worldviews present different ideals, with differing visions for public life as well. Differing visions lead to differing realities.[2]

Even our Constitution grounds the rights and freedoms of individuals not in the will of man but in the will of the Creator. As I've heard it said, "Democracy is two wolves and a lamb voting on what to have for lunch. Liberty is the lamb having grounds, before God, on which to contest the vote."

There must be something more than the voice of the majority.

It is the voice of God speaking through creation and in his Word (Ps. 19).

This is why, when Martin Luther King Jr. took his courageous stand, he had the power to say that the American majority was wrong in how it treated black men and women, even though racism had been codified into law. It was supported by the majority of American citizens. And yet Dr. King said these laws violated a higher law, the law of the Creator. On that basis he called America to repentance.

When our society encourages us to leave our Christian convictions out of the public square, we must reply that we cannot. And had generations of Christians before us done that, we would be living in a country with far fewer freedoms.

The new humanity created by the gospel has implications for all of life, so we've got to apply the gospel to all of life.

But we must be equally careful here by going so far as to say particular policy prescriptions bear God's authority. For example, biblically, we know that we must care about the poor. We also know that God has given to individual men and women the dignity and initiative to provide for themselves. We can and should teach both. But assessing how well a particular welfare policy balances those two principles, in most cases, goes beyond the scope of the church's teaching responsibility. It is an exercise in applied wisdom, not in applying clear biblical teaching.

From the pulpit we can and should present biblical ideals that have implications for public policies. But those of us in church leadership should also, in most cases, refrain from endorsing particular policies and candidates. In most cases, we deal with the *ideal*, which is foundational, not the policy, which is derivative.

God's Word never errs.

Whatever he says is good *is good*.

Whatever he declares unjust *is unjust*.

But while Scripture provides wisdom applicable to every issue—economics, family life, education, environment, etc.—it does not speak with equal clarity on which current strategies best address each issue or best promote the general welfare. It is one thing to say the Bible is abundantly relevant for economic policy, for example. It is another to say that the Bible is sufficient and exhaustive for twenty-first-century American economic questions.

When it comes to things like empowerment for the poor, the best strategies to address racial injustice, or the most responsible ways to steward the environment, Christians in the same church—even the same small group—should be able to come to different conclusions and still experience unity in Christ.

This is not to say all viewpoints are equally correct.

Many policies are destructive.

Many policies protect corrupt interests.

Many policies need to be exposed as antithetical to the common good.

And you should feel free to argue your convictions on the above. But not in a way that implies you have the church's authority behind you. We should be able to disagree charitably on these things while not questioning the spirituality of those who see things differently. We should see the dividing line in the church not running between Republicans and Democrats and their respective strategies but between those who care about justice, righteousness, equity, and compassion, and those who don't. Just because someone doesn't agree with our particular strategy for promoting the general welfare doesn't mean they don't care about poverty relief.

> We should be able to disagree charitably on policy matters while not questioning the spirituality of those who see things differently.

### Myth 2: Secondary ideals are matters of first importance.

The opposite error of thinking the gospel doesn't apply to politics is elevating secondary political ideals to matters of *first* importance. This is how many people approach politics.

If you don't agree with me *on this*, then we can't have fellowship together.

Practically, they feel more at home with those who share their political bent than those who share their faith.

If that's true about us, the gospel is not above all in our hearts. Christians should feel a greater unity in Christ than they do disunity in political strategies.

One reason we need to hold our political convictions loosely is that we might be wrong about some of them. Policy always seems *so clear* to us in the moment. But even if you're well informed, years from now you're likely to realize some of your most passionately held positions were off.

I once served on a team that was charged to craft public statements on hot-button issues for a network of churches. It was 2003, right after George W. Bush, with the near-unanimous backing of Congress, declared the Iraq war. If you don't remember that time, almost *everyone* was in favor of the war.

Republicans *and* Democrats.

Certain members of our team wanted to craft a statement publicly endorsing it. I suggested that while I was personally in favor of the war at the time, believing it at that point to be justified, we ought to refrain from attaching our network's name to it. Why not instead issue a statement articulating the theory of just war and a pledge to pray for our leaders as they sought to ascertain whether this one was and the wisdom to pursue it as such?

I was told that such a statement would be perceived as anemic and cowardly. In the end the team voted 9–0 in favor of endorsing the Iraq war. There was one abstention—from a guy too conflicted to vote in favor but still too cowardly to stand his ground and vote against the committee.

Yes, that was me.

Now, fifteen years later, it is clear we should have shown more restraint. There were a lot of things we didn't know then. But the rightness of the war just seemed *so clear* to everyone at the time.

That's the problem.

In the church we are neither called nor competent to adjudicate the finer details of policy. And what is really tragic is when we tie the church's authority, and reputation, to those things.

I might be wrong about which war is just or which economic strategy is most effective. But I'm not wrong about the gospel. So if I speak with the same level of authority on politics that I do Scripture, I shouldn't be surprised when I find my gospel platform diminishes.

Now, to be clear, I don't *think* I'm wrong about my political views. If I did, I'd change them (so would you, I hope!). But hopefully I've got enough humility to admit that my political vision isn't twenty-twenty. But I am confident I see the gospel clearly.

As I often tell my church, I may be wrong about my position on global warming, but I know I'm not wrong about the gospel. I never want my opinion on the former to prevent people from hearing the latter.

The bigger problem, though, isn't even that we may be right or wrong.

The biggest problem is that even if we *are* right in our position on an issue, politics simply doesn't matter as much as the gospel. What do we want to be known for in our churches—political policies or gospel preaching?

I don't even want things that I am *right* about to keep people from hearing me on the gospel. I have one primary message—the gospel.

And it must be above all else.

Recently I got a letter from someone who attended our church who confessed to me that she'd sniped at me several times on Twitter over things she didn't like about my beliefs. Put it this way, her Twitter handle had "left" in the name—@LeftLinda or something like that. We started a dialogue, and I reinforced to her what I want our church to be known for—the gospel. We disagreed on just about every political issue. But I told her that I didn't want our church to be about that. I'd always be clear about what the Bible said, but politics would not be a defining feature of our church.

A few months later I got a picture in the mail.

It was of Linda getting baptized at our church. She had decided to stick around, heard the gospel in her soul, and confessed faith in Christ. She was joining our church as a new sister in Christ.

I met her and her husband over lunch, and she told me how many things in her life were changing. I realized that day that if politics defined our church—if our church had the reputation of being the place where all the Republicans go and the Republican pastor sneaks in subtle talking points whenever he can—we'd never have had the chance to reach @LeftLinda with the gospel.

I choose @LeftLinda every time.

I'll still hold my political positions and champion the principles behind them, but I will do my best to keep the gospel above all.

Churches should be places where people who stridently disagree on political policy questions come together in unity in Christ.

Believe it or not, Jesus had some political drama right in his chosen circle of twelve. We know that two of Jesus' disciples were "Simon the Zealot" (Fox News) and "Matthew the Tax Collector" (MSNBC). Yes, yes, I realize that our political milieu and theirs was nothing alike—the Fox News and MSNBC thing was a joke. But those two groups had some pretty deep-seated political disagreements. Zealots were those Jews that thought Judaism should revolt against Rome, driving out all Roman influence. Tax collectors worked *for* Rome, so they represented the establishment. One thought war with Rome was the best course of action; the other thought complicity with Rome was wiser.

One wanted to stick it to the man.

The other *was* the man.

I'm sure Simon and Matthew had some interesting and incendiary political discussions by the campfires in the evening. I can just imagine Jesus watching with amusement as they went back and forth. But at the end of the day, they found in their love for Jesus a unity greater than the political questions that divided them.

Lord, let it be so again.

### Myth 3: There is never a time to take a controversial political stand.

We're charting out into deeper and deeper waters here, so hang on tight.

On one hand, the Christian worldview has ramifications for how we see everything in our lives. *See myth 1.* This certainly includes which approaches to governing people are the most just and helpful. Furthermore, Christian obedience requires that we stand up for truth, justice, and compassion, so when we see groups in our society suffering unjustly, we have to speak out.

On the other hand, we know that the church has been given a specific mission, and getting mired in the secondary questions of politics can divert our mission and mute our witness. *See myth 2.*

So how do we manage the tension between these two truths?

Let me warn you: if you're confident you know the answer, my guess is you're not living in the tension the gospel demands.

I am often asked to make public statements and sign various political petitions. The requests sometimes come from the left, sometimes from the right. And the issues others demand I endorse constantly change.

When is speaking to a specific issue a matter of faithfulness to the gospel, and when is it distraction from the gospel?

Scripture is full, after all, of admonitions for God's people to rebuke evil, sometimes with stinging specificity. Read through the prophets, and you hear God calling out injustices of all kinds.

Toward children.

Toward women.

Toward laborers.

Toward employers.

Toward the outcast, the poor, the voiceless.

And about personal moral evil, too. The prophets never tired of blasting Israel, for instance, when they indulged in sexual immorality.

The prophets trumpet a call for God's justice, but calls for justice without specific steps to redress the injustice–like we often see today–amount to little more than sentiment. Men like William Wilberforce and Martin Luther King Jr. frequently quoted from prophetic books like Amos to inspire our society to turn to justice. And they (rightly) called on their governments to institute the measures to redress the injustice.

In the New Testament, John the Baptist preached a "baptism of repentance," complete with specific accusations about the ways God's people–and the local rulers–were disobedient to God's law. He called out abuses of power carried out by soldiers and rebuked Herod for sleeping with his brother's wife. That later led to his execution. If John were around today, I imagine that a lot of Christians would have told him to keep quiet about issues of sexual morality.

*Stick to the spiritual stuff, John. Stop commenting on public sexuality.*

But what was Jesus' assessment of John's ministry?

> "Truly I tell you, among those born of women no one greater than John the Baptist has appeared." (Matt. 11:11)

The church has often failed to speak as directly and specifically as we should in the political realm concerning issues of both injustice and morality.

Dietrich Bonhoeffer lamented this about his German church in the 1930s. The church in that generation was content simply to say, "Discrimination is wrong," a statement that the Nazi Party would allow. But Bonhoeffer and the Confessing Church knew that obedience required them to take another step, getting their hands dirty by saying, "We must oppose the Nazis."

Like John the Baptist, Bonhoeffer paid for that rebuke with his life.

In the 1850s, many Christian churches were reluctant to say anything specifically about slavery, even though they opposed the practice personally. Again in the 1960s, far too many churches stayed silent when they should have offered their hand—and their voice—to the civil rights movement.

Both of those instances are embarrassments to the church today, and rightfully so.

Today far too many churches are silent about the wickedness of abortion, the sanctity of marriage, lingering inequities in the justice system, the harms of predatory lending, and many other matters.

However, as we have already mentioned, speaking to politics too frequently (or too carelessly) can divert us from our mission and dilute our witness. The ministry of Jesus provides us with a helpful example of navigating the tension.

In Luke 12:13-14, Jesus was asked a specific social justice question: "My older brother used his 'older brother privilege' to extort money from me!" But Jesus refused to adjudicate, recusing himself with this dismissive phrase: "Man, who made me a judge . . . over you?" (ESV).

Instead, he preached a sermon on the danger of greed to both of them (Luke 12:15-21).

It's not that Jesus didn't care about the justice of this case or that he wouldn't have been able to offer wise counsel. I'm sure his judgment would have been spot on! Evidently Jesus knew that to get involved in the particulars of *this* case would take him away from his primary mission of preaching the gospel. Soon he'd have a line of people wanting him to weigh the merits of their case, and then he would no longer have the bandwidth to do the one thing he came to do: seek and save the lost.

Think about it. If Jesus began to offer judgments on individual cases, wouldn't his audience begin to be divided into "those who agreed with his judgments" and "those who didn't"? Jesus didn't want people dividing with him over that. He wanted them to divide with him, or stand with him, because of the gospel.

Throughout his ministry, Jesus showed remarkable restraint from getting involved in political and social causes. After he fed the five thousand with five loaves and two fish, for example, the people wanted to make him their political king. If this guy could do this with five loaves and two fish, imagine what he could do with the stock market! When Jesus perceived their intent, he ran away and hid in the mountains, and came back later *preaching the gospel* (John 6:15, 22–28). Even ending world hunger was a secondary matter to preaching the gospel.

We see the same restraint in the ministries of the apostles. Paul, for instance, spent relatively little time arbitrating the various social ills plaguing the Roman Empire–of which there were many!–focusing instead on spreading the gospel and planting churches. In his letters to the churches, he does not generally call believers to particular points of political advocacy. Instead, he opposes the core issues of discrimination, injustice, and intractable social hierarchy, injecting into the churches the seeds that would ultimately undo those ills in society.

Sure, principles from his letters can be applied in the public sphere. But that's the point. Paul taught his churches the principles of the kingdom in his letters but stopped short of applying them in the public square. He let individual believers from his churches do that, but he did not attach his apostolic authority or the reputation of the church to their efforts.

The more I've wrestled with this question, the more helpful it has been to recognize that the church exists in the world as both *organism* and *organization.*

As an organism, believers should permeate every part of society, bringing Scripture-shaped, gospel-infused wisdom wherever they go. We want Christians influencing business, education, health care, welfare, stewardship of the earth, taxation policies, trade, and everything in between. This is what it means for Christians to be salt and light to the world.

So let me be clear (in case I haven't been): we want to see Christians in our churches getting *more* involved in the political process, not *less*.

In fact, my hope is that many believers become so passionate about political engagement that they pursue it as a calling. A few years ago someone challenged me to make a list of "dream prayers"–huge, audacious things to ask God to accomplish through me before I died. One of the ones I wrote down was that God would raise up a Supreme Court justice from our congregation. Big, I know. My point in sharing that with you is that I am not advocating Christians get out of politics.

As an organization, however, the church must narrow its corporate involvement in these spheres. The corporate church–the institutional church–is called to teach the Word of God and make disciples. The more we tie ourselves, organizationally, to business programs, reforms in art, educational initiatives, medical advances, or specific political agendas, the more diluted we become in our mission. Good things take us away from the *one* thing. In other words, I want the church to become more *and* less involved in politics. As an organism, more; as an organization, less.

We can never remind ourselves too often that the church is the *only* body Jesus left to multiply disciples in the world.

Think of it like this.

If you're an EMT and you show up at the site of an earthquake, you're not serving others well if you roll up your sleeves and start hauling away debris or if you help a crying little girl find her lost puppy. That's all important work, but as one of the only people trained in emergency care, you should focus on doing that. It's why you were called to the site.

That's how the church should think about its commission to preach the gospel. Of the thousand good endeavors the church can engage in, none is as unique as the Great Commission. As Christopher Wright says, God doesn't have a set of missions for his church; he formed a church for his mission.[3] Jesus summarized our portion of that mission in Matthew 28:18–20: make disciples. That mission must always remain primary.

I'm not advocating that we ever divorce our preaching of the gospel from good works and loving our neighbor. I think I made that clear in a previous chapter. I'm advocating that the institutional church keep its focus on the one thing Jesus commanded us to do: make disciples.

Whenever I turn on the news now, it seems like–in the few minutes since I checked it last–the world has imploded. Pundits are losing their minds over some decision by congress, some statement by the president, some verdict by the court, some acquittal given by a jury, some program by a mayor, some article in the *New York Times*. Social media has blown up with everyone signaling what side of the issue they are on and why anybody worthy of the title "human" agrees with them. And then I start getting tweets and emails demanding I publicly pick a side.

Often, as I consider whatever issue is at hand, I do see moral implications involved. And I know the issues are important.

*Oh, to speak or not to speak?*

In our land of twenty-four-hour news cycles, which sustain their profits by sensationalism and outrage, the above scenario seems to happen at least once a week.

You may not have as many people *directly* asking you to make public statements, but I'm sure you feel the same pressure to "speak out" at the right times and for the right causes. And yet you aren't always sure how to do so with wisdom, grace, and gospel focus.

Our leadership team has found two diagnostic questions to be of incredible value in helping us decide:

*First, are the facts so clear and the moral obligations so obvious that Christians cannot, in good conscience, disagree?*

Often we just can't draw a direct biblical line between a biblical mandate and a particular policy prescription. For instance, as I've stated, we know the church has a moral obligation to advocate care of the poor. That's clear. Conservatives and liberals, however, differ in the ways they think our society can best pursue this. We also teach that our government has a responsibility to protect its citizens. And we teach that we have an obligation to be merciful to those in need, which includes the immigrant and the refugee. But it is beyond the purview of the church's commission to dictate, for instance, how many refugees our nation should let in each year or the best practices for protecting our borders.

As I've explained in our church, we teach the moral obligations, but we usually refrain from divinizing specific strategies unless we can draw a straight line from the biblical text to the policy. Of course, I have my own opinions about which strategies are more effective than others, and I hope you do as well. But I confuse the issue when I suggest that the only way to care for the poor is the political method I personally subscribe to.

Pastor Matt Chandler uses a helpful analogy here. He compares our concern for the poor to a house. We should all agree on the biblical foundations of caring for the poor—justice and compassion. We should also agree on the walls that frame our house—advocacy and activism. But we can disagree about which "public policy furniture" goes where in the house. For those of us in Christian leadership, we are not typically called or competent to speak to the "furniture" piece of the puzzle. We should leave latitude for people to interpret and apply the gospel rather than putting the church's authority behind specific policies.[4]

The house will continue to stand for generations to come, but the furniture will change from generation to generation.

It's best not to tie your reputation to an ugly loveseat.

There's a huge difference between believing our position is the right one and being certain that our position is the only biblically allowable one. As a pastor, or as president of the Southern Baptist Convention, I have to show even greater restraint. When I publicly advocate certain policies, people don't hear that as, "I personally believe this policy is the wisest one," but as "This is what I declare to be the Christian position, and if you disagree, you are out of step with the church," even if I don't say that.

And, of course, there may *not* be room to disagree on a particular issue. We can and should advocate *particular* policies that preserve the sanctity of life, religious liberty, the sanctity of the home, and equal protections under the law. But in most cases we need to be sure there's a *direct* line from Scripture before we say anything about a specific political policy. If biblically faithful Christians can stand across the aisle from you on a political issue, it's probably best to shy away from that trigger.

*Second, does it rise to the level that our witness requires us, as an organization, to speak?*

Even if the morals of a particular issue are clear, sometimes endorsing a position mires us in an area outside of our calling and our institutional expertise. Jesus did not refrain from giving an opinion in Luke 12 to the brother who felt cheated because the issues were unclear to him. He did so because adjudicating that case was beyond the scope of his commission.

Other times, however, a failure to speak as an organization tarnishes the church's witness.

There is not a clear-cut grid we can use to figure out when speaking to an issue is necessary for our witness and when it's an encumbrance—it takes an understanding of the times, a dependence on the Spirit's guidance, and a willingness to change course when we perceive that advocacy (or nonadvocacy) is no longer helpful.

The writer of 1 Chronicles commended the sons of Issachar, who "had understanding of the times, and knew what Israel ought to do" (1 Chron. 12:32 ESV). That means they discerned in the issues at hand broader implications of what was happening in society. Maybe after prayer we perceive a looming danger in a societal or governmental trend, and we feel compelled to speak.

But maybe we realize that in being called upon to speak out, we are being used as a tool by one side of the culture war to beat the other, and so we choose not to speak. This happens to me a lot. To both the political left and right, the church is nothing but a handy tool for the accomplishment of their purposes.

The church should not be anybody's tool.

Tools are soon regarded as fools.

The evangelical church was wrong to sit on the sidelines during the civil rights movement saying that this was a political matter, not a gospel one. Does an ongoing commitment to civil rights demand similar advocacy for changes in the contemporary legal system, funding for education, and voting district lines? Sometimes. But sometimes getting deeply involved in these discussions (as an organization) encumbers us in particulars beyond our calling.

Does advocating for the sanctity of marriage mean supporting laws that legitimize only heterosexual unions? Does proclaiming God's designs for gender mean advocating for "bathroom bills" that require people to use only the bathroom of their birth gender? Does advocacy for the sanctity of life mean endorsement of laws that make abortion illegal in all circumstances? Does believing that God gives to people the dignity and responsibility to provide for themselves require a limited-government approach to business? Does believing that power tends to corrupt every person lead to advocacy for a smaller government with lots of checks and balances?

To some of these questions I would answer a clear yes.

For others, however, the answers are not always as clear.

If we fail to speak where we should, others will be harmed through our silence. But if we speak at the right times and in the right ways, we can save lives and promote the good of our neighbor.

A few months ago a couple came into my office unannounced, wanting to share some news with me.

"A year ago," the woman said, "you talked about the value of all human life. And you actually decried the evil of elective abortion. There was a girl listening to your sermon that day who had an appointment at Planned Parenthood later that afternoon. But after hearing your sermon, she decided to choose life. She put her baby girl up for adoption, and we were the family that adopted her. We thought you'd like to meet the little girl whose life you saved with your courageous words."

I held in my arms a baby saved by connecting the dots between a biblical principle and a political issue.

No regrets.

### Myth 4: We see everything clearly.

Great Christians can be wrong.

As a young believer, that was hard for me to accept. It can be embarrassing to go back and read about some of my English theological heroes who defended imperialism from the Bible, or American pastors who were silent on discrimination–or, even worse, accepted a "scriptural" basis for the hierarchy of the races and human slavery. Or Martin Luther who said those awful things about the Jews in his later years.

But it shouldn't be surprising. Each and every one of us is more deeply shaped by our culture than we probably realize.

By the way–small rabbit trail. This is one of the reasons we should read broadly and listen to different cultures, perspectives, and time periods. Every culture has blind spots and deficiencies, of course, but they tend to have *different* blind spots and deficiencies. Reading broadly allows thinkers from other cultures to point out some of the ways we have drunk our own culture's Kool-Aid without even knowing it.

> The most important thing to take away from the mistakes of our heroes in the past, I believe, is a posture of humility in the present.

The most important thing to take away from the mistakes of our heroes in the past, I believe, is a posture of humility in the present. Rather than shake our heads in self-righteous dismay *(How could they have been so backwards? Thank God we're so sophisticated and have it figured out!)*, we should say, "If even those great heroes of faith got some things wrong, I'd be a fool to think I've got everything right." If their sincerity was not enough to keep them from error, can we guarantee that ours will be?

Do we really think our great-grandchildren will look back at us and admire how advanced we were in our thinking, how we got everything right?

My bet is on "nope."

They likely will look back at us and wonder how we could have been so blind on some issue.

Yet my opinions feel so right, so matter-of-fact to me right now!

We would do well to prepare for that humbling moment by humbling ourselves in advance.

This is not to say, of course, that we should stop applying gospel wisdom to politics or that we should refrain from developing firm convictions. We are responsible to search out Scripture diligently, pray for wisdom, and then apply it the best way we know how. Our advocacy can make a big difference in preserving justice and promoting life. But as we seek to walk the path of gospel wisdom, we have to show restraint and allow for correction and redirection.

Chances are, those on the political right have something to learn from the left.

And those on the political left have something to learn from the right.

And I don't just mean we can "learn" how stupid *those people* are and "there, but for the grace of God, go I." I legitimately mean that we can learn more about applying the gospel to politics. Neither right nor left sees everything clearly. This is not to say we're both equally right. Just that together we can seek the Scriptures and apply the gospel *better* as we learn from each other.

When it comes to care for the poor, racial reconciliation, respect for life, freedom, religious liberty, and the dignity of all people, the dividing line in the church should not be between left and right, as if poverty relief is only a concern for those on one side of the political spectrum. The dividing line in the church is between those who care to see the poor empowered and are seeking to make that happen and those who don't.

## A UNITED CHURCH IN A DIVIDED WORLD

As Christians, our primary charge is not to transform political structures.

Our primary charge is to make disciples of all people.

We should proclaim biblical values and advocate for justice for all. We should watch out for the poor. But, like the apostles and Jesus before them, we should show restraint in how particular our advocacy is on most issues. Our gospel mission is too important. It must remain above all. So where the Bible does not draw a direct line to policy, we ought to show caution and restraint in drawing it also.

Christians alone have been given the commission to invite men and women into gospel life. The one thing Jesus told us to do was not to march on Rome (or Washington, DC), but to bring the gospel to Jerusalem, Judea, Samaria, and the ends of the earth. God help us if our political passions ever stand in the way of this supreme commission.

We need a generation of Christian leaders who will not abdicate their God-given commission for the allure of politics—who believe, like Charles Spurgeon, that to accept the role of the king of England would be a demotion in our calling.

Our time desperately needs a generation of leaders with the courage to speak out where we must and the humility to listen to other believers who see various political questions differently.

Shortly after I had accepted the call to ministry, I had a chance to sit down with a famous senator who had always been a kind of political hero to my family and me. He was in his late eighties and had been engaged in politics for decades. I told him that I had strongly considered going into politics, but God had called me into ministry.

"Oh, son," he said. "You made the right choice. Preaching the gospel to the next generation is far more important than anything I have accomplished on Capitol Hill."

God calls some people into politics, and we need to thank God for them.

We need to pray for them.

We need to advocate that they lead with justice, compassion, and wisdom.

But let us never take our eyes off our primary commission— to preach the gospel.

If we let the gospel reign above our politics, we can show our society something it desperately longs to see—a body of men and women who stand united even in the midst of differing political perspectives.

That can only happen when we see the thing uniting us as greater, bigger, better, and above all that divides us. If the church in our generation *can* demonstrate unity in the gospel that overcomes even our divisions in politics, we will shine a light that will genuinely dazzle everyone around us.

And, by God's grace, we will draw many to faith in Jesus.

# **GOSPEL**
## VICTORY

*"In spite of sorrow, loss, and pain,*
*our course be onward still; we sow on*
*Burmah's barren plain, we reap on Zion's hill."*
–Adoniram Judson

You are filling out your profile for Fakeblock, the new online social platform taking the country by storm, when this question pops up:

*What is the MOST important thing about you?*

What pops into your mind first as a response to that question? What is the thing most responsible for getting you where you are, or the one thing that will have the most shaping impact on your future? What one thing, if people knew this about you, would explain the most about how you approach life?

The school you graduated from?

How many kids you have?

Your net worth?

Your good looks?

Your athleticism?

What theologian A. W. Tozer said was the most important thing about you may not even make your top 10.

Tozer said, "What comes into our minds when we think about God is the most important thing about us."[1]

That's probably why, toward the end of his ministry, Jesus asked his disciples specifically what they thought about him.

Peter replied, "You are the Christ, the Son of the living God."

"And Jesus answered him, 'Blessed are you, Simon Bar-Jonah! For flesh and blood has not revealed this to you, but my Father who is in heaven. And I tell you, you are Peter, and on this rock I will build my church, and the gates of hell shall not prevail against it'" (Matt. 16:16–18 ESV).

Translation: If we get Jesus' identity right, deep in our bones, not even the gates of hell will be able to stop us.

The quality of our ministry is directly tied to the accuracy of our view of Jesus.

Sometimes we think "the gates of hell will not prevail against you" only means that Jesus will protect us from all of Satan's vicious attacks. But this verse is about Satan's inability to keep us from plundering his kingdom, not his inability to plunder ours.

Think about it: Are "gates" an *offensive* weapon?

When's the last time you attacked someone with a gate? How would you even do that? Beat them over the head with it?

Gates are a *defensive* weapon, designed to keep intruders out. Jesus is saying that when we confess faithfully, not only will he protect our church, but he'll also enable us to advance God's kingdom into Satan's most fortified strongholds.

In other words, *If we confess the gospel faithfully, we are going to be unstoppable.*

The battle is on—for the souls of our children, our neighbors, our nation, and our world. We hear news from the front lines of victories and defeats, advances and retreats.

*At such-and-such church, they have baptized three hundred people this year!*

*But in such-and-such state, they've had to close five hundred churches.*

*Last year more money was given to the cause of Christian mission than any previous year, even adjusting for inflation.*

*No sizable evangelical denomination is keeping up with population growth. Most are shrinking.*

Glancing around at the map, it can be difficult to know which way the war is headed.

Until we remember that the battle is already won.

Jesus never promised that he would protect the rear guard of Christians as they managed a slow retreat into obscurity. He never urged us to pray, "God, protect our families while our society spirals into chaos."

Rather, he promised us that if we'd be faithful in our confession, he'd lead us deeper and deeper into enemy territory. No weapon formed against us will prosper. All those who rise up against us will fall. The victory only *looks* uncertain to us. But the strongholds of Satan were eternally crushed at Calvary.

So we now fight *from* victory, not *for* it.

This reminds me of a story about Abraham Lincoln.

When the Union Army pushed the Confederates back into Richmond, one of Lincoln's generals burst into his cabinet meeting and said, "President Lincoln, I am pleased to tell you we have finally pushed the enemy out of our territory and back into his own."

Lincoln said to the other generals in the room, "When will my generals learn that the whole country is our territory?"

Jesus is not content to be Lord of the church.

He died to be Lord of the whole earth.

*If we confess the gospel faithfully, we are unstoppable.*

There are still four thousand unreached people groups with no witness.

There are communities of refugees displaced around the globe.

There are populations of prisoners that need a gospel witness.

There are foster kids that need a home.

There are single mothers in need of community.

There are homeless men and women in need of shelter.

Some of your friends need Jesus.

Are we sufficient for the task? Like Ezekiel, standing overwhelmed before the valley of dry bones, we confess our complete and utter inability for the task. But we know the Spirit of God can do through us all that he has determined. We know that God will breathe life into our work. We know we will see spiritual resurrection.

He promises to bring dead souls to life.

He promises his Word will not return void.

Be careful. God only blesses those who go forward in confidence, never those who huddle back in fear. The church is not composed of "those who shrink back and are destroyed, but of those who have faith" (Heb. 10:39 ESV). Those who shrank back in Joshua's day were destroyed. Those who shrink back in ours will be also.

There's only one way the church succeeds:

Aggressively forward.

So, instead of adopting a defensive, intimidated posture toward the world, trying only to hold on to what we have and protect it from the enemy, we must again go on the offensive. It's time to burn the ships and send out believers to besiege the gates of hell.

Without the power of the gospel, the gates will never budge.

With the power of the gospel, they are as flimsy as tissue paper.

So say it with me: *I confess that* . . .

Jesus is the Lord of the whole earth, the King of kings and Lord of lords.

He is the Messiah, the Christ, the Son of the living God, the one way of salvation for all people, the one name under heaven given among men whereby we must be saved.

Whoever will call upon the name of the Lord will be saved.

There is no difference in the Jew and the Greek, the black and the white, the rich and the poor, the Democrat and the Republican. Since the beginning of time, there's only been one race of human—sinner—and one Savior, Jesus.

The same Lord is Lord of all, bestowing his riches on whoever calls upon him. He is not willing that any should perish but that all should come to repentance.

I confess this because the Bible Jesus authorized teaches it, and I believe that all Scripture is given by inspiration of God. Whether or not that gospel confession is popular, it is the power of God—and that's the last thing I want to lose.

*If we confess the gospel faithfully, we are unstoppable.*

And, because of Jesus' promise that he puts on this confession, we will never be satisfied when there is such lostness in our community and our world.

The whole country is his territory!

People ask me, "Aren't there enough churches already? When are Christians going to stop trying to plant more of them?"

When Jesus comes back or the last person on planet earth gets saved.

That's my answer.

Hell doesn't rest.

Neither will I.

Jesus is not done.

Neither are we.

# NOTES

## Chapter 1: Gospel above All

1. Timothy Keller, *The Prodigal God* (New York: Penguin, 2011), 128.

## Chapter 2: Gospel Change

1. https://www.christianitytoday.com/news/2018/september/china-bans-zion-beijing-house-church-surveillance-ezra-jin.html

2. Nathan Cole, "Spiritual Travels," *William and Mary Quarterly* 7 (1950): 591.

3. Iain Murray, ed., C. H. Spurgeon Autobiography: *The Early Years 1834–1859* (London: Banner of Truth, 1962), 87–90.

## Chapter 3: Gospel Mission

1. Robert Coleman, *The Master Plan of Evangelism* (Grand Rapids: Revell, 2010), 104.

2. "Study: Churchgoers Believe in Sharing Faith, Most Never Do," LifeWay Research, January 2, 2014, accessed February 18, 2019, https://lifewayresearch.com/2014/01/02/study-churchgoers-believe-in-sharing-faith-most-never-do.

3. Rosaria Butterfield, *The Gospel Comes with a House Key: Practicing Radically Ordinary Hospitality in Our Post-Christian World* (Wheaton: Crossway, 2018), 63.

4. Tim Keller, *Generous Justice: How God's Grace Makes Us Just* (New York: Penguin, 2012).

5. Alan Noble, *Disruptive Witness: Speaking Truth in a Distracted Age* (Downers Grove, IL: InterVarsity Press, 2018), 2.

6. Ben Sasse, *Them: Why We Hate Each Other—and How to Heal* (New York: St. Martin's Press, 2018), 185.

7. Noble, *Disruptive Witness*, 2.

8. Justin Taylor, "How Much Do You Have to Hate Somebody to Not Proselytize?," The Gospel Coalition, November 18, 2009, accessed February 18, 2019, https://www.thegospelcoalition.org/blogs/justin-taylor/how-much-do-you-have-to-hate-somebody-to-not-proselytize.

9. *NIV Zondervan Study Bible*, eBook: *Built on the Truth of Scripture and Centered on the Gospel Message* (Grand Rapids: Zondervan, 2015), Kindle Edition, 269835-269838).

### Chapter 4: Gospel Multiplication

1. Stephen Neill, *A History of Christian Missions* (Harmondsworth, UK: Penguin, 1986), 22.

2. Leonard Lyons, *Washington Post, Loose-Leaf Notebook,* January 30, 1947, Washington, DC, 9.

3. Rodney Stark, *The Rise of Christianity: How the Obscure, Marginal Jesus Movement Became the Dominant Religious Force in the Western World in a Few Centuries* (San Francisco: Harper Collins, 1997), 3.

### Chapter 5: Gospel Hope

1. Sean T. Collins, "Carrie Fisher's 10 Greatest 'Star Wars' Moments," *Rolling Stone*, December 27, 2016, accessed February 18, 2019, https://www.rollingstone.com.

2. D. Martyn Lloyd-Jones, "Revival: An Historical and Theological Survey," in *The Puritans: Their Origins and Successors; Addresses Delivered at the Puritan and Westminster Conferences 1959–1978* (Carlisle, PA: Banner of Truth Trust, 1987), 18.

3. Ibid.

4. Ibid.

5. Jonathan Edwards, Edwards on Revivals: Containing a Faithful Narrative of the Surprising Work of God (New York: Dunning & Spalding, 1832), 48.

6. Tim Keller, "Revival: The Need for Gospel Renewal" December 19, 2014, https://www.faithgateway.com/need-gospel-renewal/#.XIQyGFNKjfY.

7. The Daily Wire, "John MacArthur/The Ben Shapiro Show Sunday Special Ep. 29," YouTube video, 1:09, December 2, 2008, https://www.youtube.com/watch?v=F-ofKxfYqGw.

8. Ben Sasse, *Them: Why We Hate Each Other—and How to Heal* (New York: St. Martin's Press, 2018), 93.

### Chapter 6: Gospel Grace

1. Raymond C. Ortlund, *The Gospel: How the Church Portrays the Beauty of Christ* (Wheaton, IL: Crossway, 2014), 17.

2. Ibid., 21.

3. Mark Dever, *The Church: The Gospel Made Visible* (Nashville, TN: B&H Academic, 2012).

4. "Big Drift" sermon delivered by Andy Stanley at North Point Community Church, 2011, https://open.life.church/items/164645-message-mp3.

5. Mindy Kaling, *Is Everyone Hanging Out without Me? (and Other Concerns)* (London: Ebury Press, 2013), 116.

6. www.goodreads.com/quotes/163531-no-man-who-is-resolved-to-make-the-most-of

7. Martin Luther King Jr., "Letter from a Birmingham Jail," in *Milestone Documents in African American History* by Paul Murray, (Amenia, NY: Salem Press, 2017).

### Chapter 7: Gospel above My Culture

1. Even as I write this, a representative from the state of Iowa has been in the headlines for questioning what is so wrong about phrases like "white nationalism" and "white supremacy."

2. Joe Helm, "Recounting a Day of Rage, Hate, Violence and Death," *Washington Post*, August 14, 2017, accessed February 19, 2019, https://www.washingtonpost.com/graphics/2017/local/charlottesville-timeline?utm_terms=.7edftc904a16.

3. www.nytimes.com/2018/03/09/us/blacks-evangelical-churches.html

4. M. Scott Peck, *The Road Less Traveled: A New Psychology of Love, Traditional Values, and Spiritual Growth* (New York: Touchstone, 2002), 120–30.

5. Albert R. Mohler Jr., "Conceived in Sin, Called by the Gospel: The Root Cause of the Stain of Racism in the Southern Baptist Convention," in *Removing the Stain of Racism from the Southern Baptist Convention: Diverse African American and White Perspectives* by Kevin M. Jones and Jarvis J. Williams (Nashville, TN: B&H Academic, 2017).

6. Martin Luther King Jr., "Letter from a Birmingham Jail."

7. Author heard this in person from Dr. Yancey.

8. Alan Cross, "Vance Pitman Podcast Interview: Church for the City and the Nations among Us," *SBC Voices* (audio blog), February 14, 2017, accessed February 19, 2019, https://sbcvoices.com/vance-pitman-podcast-church-for-the-city-and-the-nations-among-us.

## Chapter 8: Gospel above My Preferences

1. G. K. Chesterton, *The Thing* (London: Sheed & Ward, 1957).

## Chapter 9: Gospel above My Politics

1. Abraham Kuyper: *A Centennial Reader*, ed. James D. Bratt (Grand Rapids: Eerdmans, 1998), 488.

2. Thomas Sowell, *A Conflict of Visions* (New Delhi: Affiliated East-West Press, 1988).

3. C. J. H. Wright, *The Mission of God* (Downers Grove, IL: IVP Academic, 2006).

4. Talk given at *Thrive* conference by Matt Chandler, Epiphany Church, Philadelphia, October 2018.

## Conclusion: Gospel Victory

1. A. W. Tozer, *The Knowledge of the Holy: The Attributes of God: Their Meaning in the Christian Life* (New York: Walker, 1996), 5.

"I've been using the CSB in sermons consistently for over a year. I love how it handles many difficult passages exceptionally well while also being exceptionally readable. *Accuracy and readability—a great combo.*"

J.D. GREEAR

CHRISTIAN
STANDARD
BIBLE®

*Accurate. Readable. Shareable.*
**Learn more at CSBible.com**

# ALSO BY
# J.D. GREEAR

## GOSPEL:
Recovering the Power that Made
Christianity Revolutionary
*J.D. Greear*
Greear shows how moralism and
legalism have often eclipsed the
gospel, even in conservative churches.
The book provides an applicable,
exciting vision of how God will use you
to bring His healing to the world.

9781433673122 **$16.99**

*Bible study also available*

## GOSPEL:
The 90-Day Devotional
*J.D. Greear*
A 90-day reminder that we never move
past the gospel; it is the beginning,
middle, and end of what God has given
to save us and make us more like Christ.

9781535934657 **$16.99**

**PUBLISHING**

# ALSO BY
# J.D. GREEAR

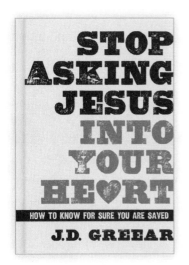

### STOP ASKING JESUS INTO YOUR HEART

Greear unpacks the doctrine of assurance, showing that salvation is a posture we take to the promise of God in Christ, a posture that begins at a certain point and is maintained for the rest of our lives.

9781433679216 **$12.99**

*Bible study also available*

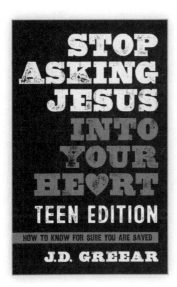

### STOP ASKING JESUS INTO YOUR HEART TEEN EDITION

The teenage years are a pivotal time in the faith journey of countless people. In this book, J. D. Greear repackages the same great content about assurance of salvation for teenagers.

9781462779215 **$9.99**

*Bible study also available*

**ALSO AVAILABLE:**
Jesus, Continued 9780310337768
Not God Enough 9780310337775
Gaining by Losing 9780310533955

PUBLISHING